# Financial Invigoration for the Average Joe

Kurtis A. Solberg

ISBN 0-7414-3479-2

*Published by:*

INFINITY
PUBLISHING.COM

*1094 New DeHaven Street, Suite 100*
*West Conshohocken, PA 19428-2713*
*Info@buybooksontheweb.com*
*www.buybooksontheweb.com*
*Toll-free (877) BUY BOOK*
*Local Phone (610) 941-9999*
*Fax (610) 941-9959*

*Printed in the United States of America*

*Printed on Recycled Paper*

*Published December 2006*

# Contents

# INTRODUCTION

Oh no, not another financial guide! Some people literally cringe at the sight of them. Have you ever tried to read a book cover-to-cover like *The Intelligent Investor* by Benjamin Graham? It's mind-numbing! Don't get me wrong, Benjamin Graham was a financial genius, but the average person is not interested in reading such complex material. That's why I chose to write this book. I take great satisfaction in educating people about personal finance in easy to understand terms.

Everyone dreams of attaining a lavish lifestyle at some point in their life. Is it possible for the average person? You bet. But it takes a little bit of effort, understanding, and organization. This book will guide you through your own financial odyssey and provide you with the opportunity to grow your personal pot of gold.

So why should you listen to me? Although I've lived a short life compared to most, I consider myself an investing entrepreneur. I have studied great investors, such as Peter Lynch and Warren Buffett, and adopted some of their techniques to create my own investing style. I've also been a certified financial specialist for the U.S. Navy for nearly nine years. Thousands of military members struggle with their finances and find themselves in situations that require positive intervention from people like me. It's my duty to share my knowledge with you, so that you can benefit from your financial situation. Even if you only take one piece of advice, or learn a new tip, I will consider this book a success.

Did you know that the average American consumer is over $8,000 dollars in debt? Not so long ago, I was one of those people. I lived paycheck to paycheck and struggled every month to pay my bills. I was a Seaman in the Navy, and an old Master Chief took me under his wing because he knew that money was a major issue for me. I was responsible, like most people are, but I never had any money. Master Chief sent me to a class called *How to be a Millionaire on a Navy Paycheck*.

That class awakened me and I discovered things like compound interest, stocks, bonds, and mutual funds. Suddenly, I was reading everything I could get my hands on about investing. Dollar signs filled my thoughts, and my main priority in life was to pay off my debt and start investing. It changed my entire outlook on life.

Most people don't even start thinking about saving for retirement until they are approaching it. Would you rather buy those Pearl Jam concert tickets with backstage passes, or deposit $200 into your retirement account? Most people would choose option A. You'll often hear people say that they would rather live for the moment. But, eventually, the moment for retirement will come and they won't be able to afford to live the lifestyle they've grown accustomed to.

So many people are scared to death to invest in the stock market. Who can blame them? You hear horror stories about the crash of 1929, the sudden drop in 1987, and the internet technology bubble burst in early 2000. But, is the stock market getting a bad rap? Absolutely! Over time, the stock market has returned an average of about 12 percent a year. You will not find a better long-term investment than the stock market. Sure, it's possible to lose money, but you can diversify your investments in such a way to lessen the risks.

Throughout this book, I'm going to guide you to financial freedom. You'll learn about everything from good debt to bad debt, creating a successful budget, investing your first dollar, and managing your new portfolio. Use this book as a stepping stone and utilize other resources to help you become more financially aware. Challenge yourself to learn something new instead of eating M&Ms on the couch and watching American Idol.

Investing takes discipline and will become habit once you start. Albert Einstein once said that compound interest is the Eighth Wonder of the World. If you have the desire to live within your means and learn about successful investment strategies, you will achieve great levels of wealth within your lifetime. Educate yourself, polish your money management skills, and build your own eighth wonder of the world through compound interest and time.

# CHAPTER 1
# FINANCIAL SUICIDE

During my own financial odyssey, I learned the term "financial suicide." *Financial suicide* is when you have no idea what's going on with your finances, and you are so far in debt that you can't even pay your bills on time. People who commit financial suicide live paycheck to paycheck and let the ATM machine balance their checkbook. Money is never saved and their debt is constantly increasing. Sound familiar? I was that guy 10 years ago. We don't commit financial suicide on purpose, but it can happen to anyone who isn't financially savvy about their situation.

Perhaps we can blame our educational system. Apparently, it's more important to learn about complex chemical formulas in chemistry class than to know how to create a budget or balance a checkbook. Write your Congressman!

Most people in our society live a high-consumption lifestyle. We are obsessed with toys. Everyone wants the latest and greatest iPOD or a 52-inch plasma television. Every aspect of our being revolves around possessions. My mother used to say that some people don't even have a pot to piss in, but they have a satellite dish. Is that true or what? I would freak out if I didn't own every single Pink Floyd CD.

There are three factors that force people into committing financial suicide:

1. **Compulsive buying**
2. **Not living within your means**
3. **Failure to track every purchase**

If you consistently commit any one of these actions, you will soon find yourself in financial hell. It seems like it would be so easy to avoid these mistakes, but millions of people unknowingly make these errors every day.

*Compulsive buying* is when you purchase something without planning on it. For example, you may have plans to go out with your friends for dinner and a movie, but as you're walking through the mall you notice a rainbow-colored Speedo that you just have to have. You instantly whip out that Visa credit card, with a 19.2 percent interest rate, and buy it on the spot.

Compulsive buying can devastate your budget. Money that was supposed to be set aside for a new car or tuition is now going towards something that was unplanned. We all have to exert some discipline and plan on making major purchases. If you have problems controlling this urge, set aside a "compulsive buying allotment" every month.

Learn your personal compulsive buying triggers. It's important that you try to avoid putting yourself in situations where compulsive buying is likely to occur. If you compulsively buy expensive electronics every time you go to Best Buy, don't go there unless you are picking up something specific that you planned on.

*Not living within your means* is a style of living beyond your budget. If you're rolling in a new Cadillac Escalade with $800 a month payments, and you can only afford $400 payments, you are definitely not living within your means. Opt for the Ford Explorer instead. Your friends and family may not be as impressed, but who cares? Wouldn't you rather have an extra $400 a month to live off of?

I can't begin to tell you how many people I have counseled about this in the Navy. Many of these young adults have never had a steady paycheck until they joined the military. They get suckered into contracts at used car dealerships and become so in debt that they're forced to use payday loan business services. Once you get into the payday loan habit, it's difficult to pull yourself out.

It's important to remember that if you find yourself going deeper into debt on a monthly basis, you're not living within your means. Curb some of those non-essential expenditures. Do you really need HBO and Showtime? I know The Sopranos can be addictive, but they aren't worth an extra $15 dollars a month on your cable bill if you are trying to pinch pennies. Try packing a lunch rather than spending five dollars a day at McDonalds. Okay, I'm not going to mention Starbucks, but you all know where I'm going with this. Some people claim that they literally could not survive without a morning latte.

*Failure to track every purchase* can wreak havoc on your finances. A very small minority of people can actually remember everything they bought and keep a running tally of their checking account embedded in their brain. This is an impossible task for the rest of us! We need to know where our money is going at all times.

Let's say you have $500 in your checking account until next payday, and you write a $200 check for your car payment, withdraw $100 from the ATM for compulsive shopping, and buy $150 worth of groceries. Your account balance is now $50. There is a good chance that you could forget about that $200 check you wrote a week earlier and when you check your account balance on the ATM, it may not reflect that check you wrote because it hasn't cleared yet. So now you're standing in front of the ATM to check your account balance and it shows $250. Without even thinking about that check, you withdraw $100 and leave insufficient funds in your account for the check to clear.

This is a very elementary example, but the same theory still applies on a bigger scale. Most of us make many purchases throughout the pay period. It's so easy to forget about purchases if you don't track them. There are many ways you can track your purchases. Microsoft Money and Quicken are two software programs that make tracking very easy. You can also do it the old-fashioned way by writing everything down in your checkbook register. Choose whatever method is easiest for you.

You should be comparing everything you track to your bank statements or online account. Every time I make a purchase, I enter it into Quicken that night. Save every receipt! This is the most important part of tracking. Put all your receipts into your wallet or purse and use them as a reference to balance your checkbook. If you don't do this task on a daily basis or at least a few times a week, I guarantee you that you will not be able to accurately track your checking account balance. You will become overwhelmed and stop tracking your purchases all together.

It is absolutely essential that you don't commit these three financial sins if you want to become wealthy. If you are already deep in debt and want to change your ways, I'm going to discuss strategies in the next chapter that will help turn your financial picture around.

The foundation for creating wealth revolves around stability. You have to make your mind up that you are willing to exhibit control. This undertaking will never work if your financial picture is like a wild rollercoaster. It doesn't matter how old you are. You can make your mind up at any time. Great fortunes have been created in relatively short periods of time.

When your finances are under control and stable, you give your money a chance to grow. That's the name of the game. You want to put yourself in a position that gives you the opportunity to save the most money to invest. It's not like you have to be a tightwad, but you have to consistently save every month. Keep this in mind as you're reading this book.

Dedicate yourself to taking control and breaking all of your habits that lead to financial suicide. Track everything down to the penny, and learn where your money is going. Once you have mastered the art of not committing financial suicide, you are ready to get out of debt and free yourself from the credit card demons.

# CHAPTER 2
# CONTROLLING THE MADNESS

Do you remember Susan Powter from the early 1990s? She was the shaved-head fitness guru who had the famous saying of, "Stop the Insanity!" That's what I think of when I think about people in serious debt.

Sometimes people are so far in debt that they need to consolidate all their bills into a single bill. Be careful! Please read this section carefully if you are one of those people who needs to consolidate bills to regain control of their finances. Non-financially savvy people often make the mistake of using the wrong kind of agency to consolidate debt.

*Never* use a credit repair clinic! They are agencies that promise to repair your credit by ruining your credit score. They negotiate with your creditors to lower your debt and agree on new terms. You have no say in these negotiations. The credit repair clinics are trying to convince your creditors that you will not pay the bill and that they need to settle on a payment to forgive the debt. This sounds good, right? Wrong! Your financial reputation is ruined after utilizing a service like this. Plus, you're paying this company a large portion of your hard-earned money. There are literally thousands of these companies trying to take advantage of you. Don't fall victim to one of these swindlers.

I have a friend who has been paying for this mistake for years. He was on a deployment for the U.S Navy and his wife was taking care of all the family finances via power of attorney while he was gone. They were broke as a joke, as my friends and I used to say. She was so excited because she went to a credit repair clinic and all of their family bills were condensed into a low monthly payment. Their family now had a lot of extra money every month and all seemed well.

She was so happy that she promised her husband that a big surprise awaited him when he returned. They had plans of buying there first house together and could easily afford a low mortgage payment since all their bills were consolidated.

Surprise! Both of their credit scores were ruined by the time he returned home. They had no idea what they had gotten themselves into. Not only was their credit ruined, but they couldn't get approved for a home loan. The credit repair clinic convinced their creditors that they were not going to pay their debts, and negotiated a payoff balance. This destroyed their credit history. A financial mistake of this magnitude constitutes a major brain fart. That one phone call and consultation to a credit repair clinic can devastate your financial life for years.

So what are your options? Utilize the *Consumer Credit Counseling Service*. It is a nonprofit agency that helps consumers resolve debt issues. They offer one-on-one counseling services by phone or online. You and your counselor will work together to come up with a spending plan that is tailored specifically for you. A thorough action plan will be established to help you become debt-free and set you on a path of financial success.

Why don't people use this service more often? People just don't know about their benefits. Your financial obligations are combined into one monthly payment without your credit being sacrificed. Counselors are available to you 365 days a year, and 24 hours a day. Nobody else offers services like this. It's the smart choice—and the only choice you should make when it comes to controlling debt issues. The Consumer Credit Counseling Service can be reached at *(800) 873-2227* or online at *www.cccsintl.org*.

## Payday Loan Hell

All of us have seen the Money Tree commercials with the annoying caterpillar eating the dollar bills. The commercials all have catchy tunes that embed into your brain for days on end. Payday loan companies will try anything to lure you into their stores. These businesses rip you off big time! They offer you free money orders and other little perks if you utilize their services. At the same time, they hope to loan you money at extremely high interest rates. The payday loan companies make a fortune off of small loans.

People become addicted to these payday loan vendors because they find themselves in a rut. They borrow money from these scam artists and can't pay them back. So, they borrow money again to pay the tab. Once you're stuck in the payday loan cycle, it can be extremely difficult to get out. It's like being locked in a prison cell with an aggressive, muscular man named Bubba. You can't run away from him, so he always gets to have his way with you.

Payday loan vendors can be predatory. For example, payday loan vendors in Oregon charge up to 521 percent on interest and fees. There are more payday loan stores than McDonald's fast food restaurants in the state of Oregon. Many states are urging lawmakers to pass payday loan reform laws.

I would never recommend using a payday loan vendor to get money. I once worked with a guy who used to go to payday loan stores to get money for bowling, pizza, and beer. This was a weekly occurrence for him. Little did he know that he could have utilized the counselors at the Consumer Credit Counseling Service to get his spending under control.

If you find yourself in a bind for cash prior to your financial revival, ask a family member or trusted friend to help you out. Be sincere. Don't be a pain in the neck and ask them on a regular basis. This is a good way to destroy relationships and friendships. Also, there are many organizations, churches, and charities that are more than willing to help you through a tough time. The Navy Marine Corps Relief Society, for example, is an organization that helps Sailors and Marines get interest-free loans to deal with unforeseen financial emergencies. Seek help from anywhere but high-interest payday loan vendors.

## Credit Card Fiasco

Okay, I'm not going to bash the credit card companies too much here. I'm going to bash the consumers who are irresponsible credit card users. Credit cards are beneficial if used properly. We all need to establish credit by using credit cards. Credit cards help us build credit and create good FICO scores.

FICO stands for Fair Isaac Company, the corporation that developed the credit scoring program, and is a mathematical representation of your credit worthiness to lending institutions. A FICO score above 650 or so is considered good. All of us should be shooting for a FICO score of 720. High FICO scores make your life easier. You are considered to have a low risk of defaulting on a loan when your FICO score is high. In return, banks offer you lower interest rates because you are considered responsible.

Credit cards become problematic when we abuse them by not paying off the balances in full every month. Many people have a handful of credit cards and max them all out. They make minimum payments and pay high interest rates every month. Making minimum payments on your credit cards is like being stuck in quicksand. You struggle to make the payments, but you never get ahead. Your credit card balance decreases at a very slow rate. The credit card companies love it when you do this because they know it will take years and years to pay off your balance if you make minimum payments. This is what Mr. Visa is hoping for!

There are literally hundreds of credit card companies that are more than willing to send nearly every consumer pre-approval offers in the mail. They spend millions of dollars on advertising and marketing so they can attract new customers who will eventually become consumed with debt.

Credit card companies couldn't care less what your financial situation is. They want you to carry huge balances and make minimum payments forever.

Here is a list of tips to follow when dealing with credit cards:

1. *Keep only one or two major credit cards like Visa, Master Card, or Discover. Pay the balances off every month or make payments larger than the minimum until the balance is paid off.*

2. *Try to use credit cards that have a fixed APR (annual percentage rate). Variable APRs will increase your interest payments over time. Shop around for companies with low fixed rates.*

3. *Don't close accounts that you have lots of credit history with. This will damage your FICO score. If you have more than two credit cards, close the accounts with the least amount of credit history once your balance is paid off.*

4. *Utilize zero percent balance transfer offers. This is a great way to get rid of an interest payment for up to six months or so. You can transfer a balance from one card to another and close the new account once the balance is paid off while still keeping your credit history from the original card.*

5. *Use credit cards to pay monthly bills (paying the balance in full every month, of course) to build reward points or cash-back bonuses. Credit cards offer incentives to get you to use your card for purchases. Take advantage of these offers to earn things like airline miles or points towards a new car.*

6. *Don't pay annual fees for credit cards. It is a waste of money and completely unnecessary.*

7. *Watch out for introductory offers. Credit card companies will often offer introductory interest rates for limited timeframes, but will dramatically increase your interest rate once the introductory time period is over.*
8. *Never sign up for merchant credit cards. Department stores are like the level-three sex offenders of the credit card industry. They like to take advantage of the financially challenged consumer by charging them an interest rate that is much higher than traditional credit cards. Check out the annual APR for a Sears credit card and your jaw will drop.*

## Savvy Credit Card Shopping

It's important to apply with reputable credit card companies that have great customer relations and value ethical business practices. Be careful when you receive non-solicited credit card pre-approvals in the mail. Those offers are being offered to thousands of people and you may not be getting a very competitive interest rate. You should always seek a credit card with competitive interest rates.

Do your homework! Don't sign up for a credit card just because they sent you a pre-approval in the mail. You aren't that one special somebody that the credit card companies hand-picked to send a pre-approval to. The following websites are great for credit card shopping and interest rate comparison:

www.finance-portal-online.com

www.creditcards.com

www.abcguides.com/creditcards

## Grow Cobwebs on your Mailbox

Most people hate getting pre-approval offers in the mail. They are annoying and we have to make sure to shred the documents to help curb identity theft. We now have the option of not receiving unsolicited offers in the mail. Every credit card application is required to put a disclaimer within the pre-approval application that gives you the choice of opting out. Call **1-888-567-8688** to stop receiving pre-approval offers. You will still receive offers from companies you are affiliated with. I highly recommend taking advantage of this service.

## Monitor your Credit History

It's a good idea to monitor your credit history periodically. People debate about how often you should check your credit report. I always encourage people to check it at least once a year. Don't be that guy or gal who finds out about an unauthorized credit card in their name while they're applying for a mortgage. You become an instant red flag for a lender if your credit is jacked up. I always think it's amazing how someone will scour over a cell phone bill and wait on hold for an operator for 15 minutes to complain, but they won't take the time to monitor their own credit report.

You are entitled to receive one free credit file disclosure per year from all three of the credit bureaus. These credit disclosures can be downloaded at www.annualcreditreport.com. Each of the credit bureaus can be contacted individually as well. The contact information for the three credit bureaus is as follows:

**Experian**
P.O. Box 949
Allen, TX 75002-0949
1-800-682-7654

**Equifax**
P.O. Box 105873
Atlanta, GA 30348
1-800-685-1111

**Trans Union**
P.O. Box 390
Springfield, PA 19064-0390
440-779-7200

Review your credit report with a fine-toothed comb. Note any discrepancies and report them to the credit bureaus. It's important to be prepared prior to applying for a loan. If your credit score isn't so hot, don't panic. Pay your bills on time and your credit score will increase over time.

## ♠ Casino Royale ♠

Whether you play the lotto, frequent the casinos, or stamp bingo sheets with your neon daubers, you are risking your financial wellbeing. I know a few people who are responsible with their money for the most part, but everything goes out the window when they gamble. Somehow, they don't consider it gambling when they're playing with the rent money. Gambling can become addictive and devastating. It can consume every aspect of your life. Life savings can be wiped out in a matter of minutes. Good luck troll dolls will not change your fate. The house always wins.

I'm not going to preach to you about not gambling. Gambling is fun when you're responsible. There's nothing like splitting aces and hitting two blackjacks. The free drinks aren't so bad either. Set limits for yourself and avoid situations where you've had trouble in the past.

If gambling has become a problem for you, seek help from www.gamblersanonymous.com. This organization is free and the only obligation for membership is to stop gambling.

## Good Debt?

Not all debt is bad. Some debt is actually good. Obviously, you don't want to be in debt up to your eyeballs and running from a gang of loan sharks, but some debt is beneficial to you in the long run. A mortgage, for example, is good debt because you are building up equity in your home. A mortgage should be thought of as an investment rather than as debt. Student loans are also good debt. You are investing in yourself, and these loans typically carry low interest rates. Don't get discouraged if you owe a lot of money on a mortgage, or in student loans. They'll pay off for you later down the road.

# CHAPTER 3
# THE GOLDEN RULE

Perhaps the most famous words ever written about investing came from ancient times. *"A part of all you earn is yours to keep,"* is a saying made famous by George Samuel Clason. George wrote "The Richest Man in Babylon" and was inspired by the ancient Babylonian writings inscribed on clay tablets. Babylon was an ancient city made up of extremely wealthy citizens. Wealth building principles were incorporated into their culture and the majority of the population was success-oriented. The Babylonian principles still apply just as much today as they did in ancient times.

The golden rule of wealth building is to pay yourself first. Take this rule to heart. You can't go wrong in life if you pay yourself every time you earn money. This rule is part of the foundation of wealth creation. The combination of not committing any of the three financial suicide sins, and paying yourself first will set you on the path to financial freedom.

Your personal quest to financial freedom hinges on your ability to follow the basic rules of wealth creation every day. You can't slip one day and max out your credit card to buy your girlfriend a new set of DDs. It's your obligation to live within your means, pay down debt, and pay yourself every time you get paid. Everything must remain balanced and run like a well-oiled machine. Committing financial suicide one month takes away from your ability to pay yourself. An inability to follow these rules will derail your chances of becoming financially independent.

So, how much should you pay yourself? A general rule of thumb is that you should save 10 percent of everything you make. Ten percent is the minimum amount you should save. Rich people save 15 to 20 percent of their income on average. Think of that 10 percent as a bill to yourself.

I don't like to use the word 'save' because people use the term loosely. People say things like, "I should save more money," or "I need to save more money." We are better off using power words like 'pay.' The word 'pay' is an action verb that tricks your mind into believing that you need to do something now. When you need to pay for something, it generally gets paid for right away. Force yourself to believe that you need to pay yourself right now, instead of waiting to save.

I know some of you are shaking your heads right now and wondering how you can possibly save 10 percent of your income. Trust me! It's possible when you live within your means. When you pay yourself first, you make yourself survive on the remaining income. You will adapt and overcome by finding creative ways to cut costs in your life. Do you really need to go to every movie premier, or can you wait for some movies to come to DVD?

After a couple months of paying yourself 10 percent, you will become accustomed to living on your new income. You will not even notice that you're missing it. A feeling of satisfaction will consume your thoughts when you see your monthly bank statements in the mail.

A few of you may be wondering how to consistently save the same amount every month when your pay may vary. There is an easy solution to this problem. Average your income over a three to four month period and save 10 percent of the average amount. This will ensure that you're saving 10 percent of your total income over time.

## The Just in Case Fund

Now it's time to get down to the nitty-gritty of the golden rule. Your portfolio will consist of two categories: savings and investments. The first priority is to establish the savings portion of your portfolio. There is a difference between savings and investing. Savings is used for emergencies and purchases that exceed your normal budget. Investing is intended to generate growth.

Where do you put the money that you save? The first thing you need to do is save at least three months' worth of income that will serve as your emergency fund. This money should be placed in a savings account or money market account at your primary banking institution. We are not concerned with generating more income and earning large amounts of interest with this account. This account must be *liquid.* A liquid account is one in which the funds can be withdrawn at any time and are easily accessible.

Your emergency fund will be available to you if you get laid off of work or your Great Aunt Edna suddenly dies, and you need to fly to London to attend the funeral services. Don't dip into this fund unless it's absolutely essential. The point of the emergency fund is to help you get through unforeseen circumstances that cause financial hardship.

Saving three months' worth of income will allow you to survive at a level you're already accustomed to without going into panic mode. You need to save enough money to cover all your regular bills and spending habits. If you feel like you need to save more than three months' worth, go ahead. Nobody knows your spending habits better than you.

## Short-term Savings

After your emergency account is fully funded, it's time to focus on your short-term savings. Short-term savings plans include things like vacations, Christmas presents, and a new turbocharger for your car. This money will also be deposited into a liquid account. You don't want to get caught off guard with these purchases. People often put these kinds of purchases onto a credit card. We want to be prepared and have the foresight to know that these purchases wait on the horizon.

This account varies from the emergency account because you should always be contributing to your short-term savings. We always have things that we want to buy. Life would be boring if we just saved money and never spent any of it. The short-term savings account enables you to be ahead of the game. You should always save enough money in the account to pay for your next purchase in full.

Your short-term savings account should also be liquid. I recommend a regular saving account for this. I put my short-term savings into a regular savings account and my emergency fund into a money market account. You can put them in the same account, but they're easier to keep track of if you separate them.

It's important to remember that you need to save for things that you want prior to purchasing them. Think of it like giving a loan to yourself. You'll make periodic withdrawals and then replenish your cash resource.

Don't get too carried away with this account. This account is not meant to grow in value and you shouldn't be depositing a lot of money into it because you're not earning good interest rates. Deposit a sufficient amount to cover upcoming purchases from three months to a year. Short-term savings are designed to help alleviate the need for credit cards.

## Long-term Savings

Long-term savings are very similar to short-term savings, except that you are looking to get some growth out of the account. This account covers periods of one year or longer. Things like mortgage down payments, bedroom sets, and a new Harley to go along with your mid-life crisis would be examples of long-term savings plans. Long-term savings should be deposited into *low-risk accounts*. A low risk account is an account that gives you a guaranteed rate of return and has a very low risk of losing money.

Some of you may be thinking that the last statement doesn't make any sense. How can you have a guaranteed rate of return and have a low risk of losing money? Governments, companies, and organizations can guarantee your money, but if they go bankrupt, or the country dives into a deep depression, the guarantee is out the window. Don't let that little fact discourage you. The chances of that happening are extremely remote. The financial system of today is much more efficient than it was during the Great Depression years. There are many checks and balances installed to ensure that similar events don't take place again.

Some examples of low-risk accounts include certificates of deposit (CDs) and U.S. savings bonds. A *bond* is a debt instrument issued for a period of time greater than one year with the purpose of raising capital by borrowing. A bond is an IOU to pay back principal plus interest. These types of accounts aren't liquid. They have penalties associated with them for early withdrawal. But, you don't need to worry about these penalties because you won't be withdrawing anything out of these accounts prior to the grace period expiring.

If you plan on buying your first home five years from now, start putting your money into five-year CDs at your bank. Stagger the length of the CDs as you get closer to the five-year mark. Refer to chapter six for guidance on creating a CD ladder. The point is not to be concerned about the liquidity of your long-term savings. Your short-term savings and your emergency fund keep your long-term savings safe.

Here's a hypothetical scenario on how to develop a savings plan:

**Table 3-1 Joe Schmoe's Savings Plan**

**Current Monthly Income** = $3,000
**Mandatory 10% Savings** = $300
Rent = $900
Credit Card Balance $4600/Payment = $150
Child Support = $400
Car Payment/Insurance = $400
Utilities/Cable/Cell Phone = $300
Medical/Dental Coverage = $150
Food = $200
Entertainment = $200
**Current Monthly Obligations Total** = $2,700

**Step 1**: Combine the $150 credit card payment with the $300 monthly savings until credit card is paid off. Joe will have his credit card paid off in about 11 months.

**Step 2**: Open a money market account and deposit the $300 mandatory savings, plus the old $150 credit card payment a month until the emergency account reaches $9,000. It will take Joe one year and eight months to save $9,000.

**Step 3**: Stop contributing to the emergency fund money market and open a savings account. Create short-term savings goals. Joe wants to ditch his girlfriend and go on a $1500 Vegas vacation with his irresponsible friends. Save that $450 for about four months. Joe now has $1800 saved after four months.

**Step 4**: Decrease savings deposits into short-term savings account from $450 to $150. Create long-term savings goals. Joe needs $3,500 for a down payment on a new car in 2 years. Deposit $300 a month for one year into 1-year CDs. Withdraw the money as the CDs mature and reinvest them into shorter term CDs until the money is needed for the down payment.

**Step 5**: Continue to contribute money to your short and long-term savings and adjust amounts as needed. Start a retirement account! We will discuss retirement accounts in detail in chapter six.

Let's recap for a minute here. You should establish an emergency fund savings account with three months of liquid income, start a short term savings money market account, and save for the long-term with CDs or U.S. savings bonds. Once your short-term and long-term savings accounts are well established, focus on saving for your retirement while simultaneously replenishing your short-term and long-term savings accounts. This series of events will help set a clear path on your journey to financial freedom. You'll never achieve financial freedom unless you live by the Babylonian principle of keeping a portion of everything you earn.

**Table 3-2 Savings Organization**

| **Account Type** | **Amount** | **Where to put money** |
|---|---|---|
| Emergency Fund | 3 months' Income | Money Market |
| Short-Term Savings | Personal Preference | Savings Acct. |
| Long-Term Savings | Personal Preference | CDs/Bonds |

# CHAPTER 4
# ORGANIZING YOUR FINANCIAL PICTURE

We're now entering the anal phase of the book where I have to crack the whip and make sure you know how to organize your finances. A lack of organization can cause extreme headaches. This section is an extension of financial sin number three (failure to track every purchase). Organizing your finances can literally be a maze. There are revolving bills, checking accounts, savings accounts, money market accounts, and investment brokerage accounts to deal with. Combine all this information with a budget and you have one giant cluster with the potential of erupting into financial sin number three. We're going to discuss how to make it easy to track all of this information without pulling your hair out.

## Budget 101

First of all, traditional budgets suck! They don't work for most people because they aren't that disciplined. Who wants to limit their spending to the penny on specific things? I sure as hell don't. Obviously, we have to budget for all of our revolving bills like rent and insurance. However, there is an outstanding alternative. Normally, budgets assign certain values to how much you can spend on certain categories. For an example, somebody may budget themselves $200.00 a month for entertainment. Instead of assigning spending values for specific categories, pay for all your bills and savings first, and then do whatever you want to with the leftover money.

It's basically the same as creating a budget, except you don't feel like your being constrained. People fail to stick with budgets because they go over their spending limits and stray away from the master plan. A complete budget is time-consuming to maintain. Maybe you want to splurge on entertainment one month and another month you'll spend nothing in this category. When you pay for your regular bills and savings first, it doesn't matter what you have left over because everything is already paid for. Budget your revolving bills and savings. The money left over is all for you. Your 10 percent savings rule is giving you the opportunity to spend money more freely because you are already allotting for emergencies and upcoming expenditures.

It's important to remember that you must incorporate living within your means along with this strategy. Your revolving bills and savings need to be lower than your income. This seems obvious, but millions of people go deeper and deeper into debt every month because they fail to live within their means. Do yourself a favor and leave some breathing room in your budget.

## Create an Umbrella

If you haven't already noticed, I highly recommend having a checking account, savings account, money market, and a brokerage account. A sound financial plan requires the use of all of these accounts. I've talked to many people who have multiple accounts at different banks. They'll have a money market through one bank, a brokerage account through a different institution, and two or three checking accounts. Why not combine all of these accounts under the same institution? Doesn't it make sense to have one financial institution handle all your finances? Multiple accounts at different institutions create a paperwork nightmare.

Most credit unions will give consumers the opportunity to set up all of the accounts I mentioned above. You don't have to worry about receiving an abundance of bank statements in your mailbox. The consolidation of your accounts creates a more even playing field. You can watch everything all at once like an offensive coordinator in the NFL. Offensive and defensive coordinators have the advantage of sitting high up in a stadium so they can view the entire field of play. They develop strategies based on what transpires on the field. You have the same advantage when you umbrella all of your accounts under one institution. You're essentially alleviating the task of simultaneously juggling multiple accounts throughout multiple institutions.

## Russian Roulette

Almost everyone has heard of the game the Russians made famous called 'Russian roulette.' It's a nerve-wracking interrogation tactic that involves a six-shot revolver handgun and five rounds of ammunition. The cylinder is loaded with five rounds of ammunition, leaving one slot open. The cylinder is then spun, and the hammer is cocked while the victim is staring down the barrel of the gun, anxiously awaiting his fate. The victim has a one in six chance of surviving and feels powerless.

I like to think of revolving bills like a six-shot revolver. These bills will catch you off-guard if you don't pay attention and you will feel like you're staring down the barrel of a revolver in a game of Russian roulette. You have to know the intimate details of all your revolving bills. So many people don't keep track of their monthly obligations and they either forget about them, or get caught off-guard when these bills show up in the mailbox.

To circumvent the effects of revolving bills, I recommend keeping detailed files of these bills. Your entire budget is based on your revolving bills and it's absolutely imperative that you know when the bills are due, how much you owe, and what percentage of your take home pay is being forfeited to these bills. This information is essential because you need to have a ballpark figure of what you owe each and every month. Obviously, some bills vary, but you can estimate the approximate value you owe each and every month.

You should create individual bill files and keep them in a safe place. It's a good idea to pick up a fireproof safe or filing cabinet and keep all the information together in one place. Monthly statements, customer service contact information, and billing addresses are all examples of what you should create in these files. I recommend placing all your mail into an incoming mail folder and filing individual statements into the filing cabinet once a month. All of your bills need to be organized in a manner so that you know when all of them are due. When revolving bills go undocumented, the road to financial sin number three will glow like a neon light.

As I mentioned before in chapter one, software programs like Microsoft Money or Quicken can help you organize your revolving bills and save you many painstaking hours of trying to keep track of this information. Don't become the victim of a game of Russian roulette with your creditors; focus on turning the tables and becoming the interrogator. Be in control and always know which bill is due next. A professional chess player can foresee the outcome of the game up to 20 moves in advance. If you want to take control of your finances, you need to foresee the creditor's next move and keep the game organized like chess-master Bobby Fischer.

## Sacrificial Lamb

This is the point of your financial journey where you need to make some sacrifices. Your finances need to allow you the flexibility to pay all of your revolving bills, save 10 percent of your income, and leave you a small cushion to buy whatever the hell you want every month. I know it's easier said than done to put yourself in this kind of position.

You're going to be forced to change things. I can guarantee you that each and every one of us can cut an unnecessary expenditure out of our budget. Do you notice how I keep referring back to financial sins? They seem like such simple rules, but those three little rules can destroy your financial picture if you don't follow them religiously. It's not like you have to live your life on the edge, constantly worrying about your finances. You just need to create habits that help curb the chances of you committing financial sins.

Find out how much money you're spending on fast food, vending machines, and at convenience stores. Often, I see people buy expensive brands instead of the generics. I know you don't want to be that cheap guy who buys the 25 cent soda at Wal-Mart, but sometimes it's necessary to lower your expenses by any means available. Price comparisons can also help you lower expenses. The Lover's Package may have your leather bondage suit for $50.00 cheaper than your favorite mall outlet store.

## Downgrade with Style

So what do you do if you've found an area in your life where you're spending way too much money? It's not always easy to just drop everything all at once and stop wasting money. A lot of people tend to spend too much on vehicles or rent. Others spend too much money on toys like video games, cell phones, or clothes. Everyone has different interests and varying spending habits. The important thing to do is to dial in on where the majority of the money is going to. If your car is costing you a grand fortune every month, trade it in for a model that is a couple of years older. The chances are very good that you'll find a comparable model with everything you want for a lot cheaper price. You can still be rolling on your 20 inch rims, blasting your new Yanni CD.

If you're stuck in a lease, take on a roommate to help ease the pain or talk to the manager about cancelling a lease early. Managers will often work with tenants even though they are under a contract. They are in the customer satisfaction industry and are eager to please in most cases. Renters can often pay a small fee to terminate their lease.

Things like insurance can also be lowered by just making a phone call. Tell your insurer that you've received better offers in the mail and that you're going to switch to one of their competitors unless they work with you. It can be very beneficial for you to be aggressive with your creditors at times. The insurance industry is very competitive and many companies will be flexible to keep your business.

Downgrading doesn't have to be negative. Start with your biggest expenses and work your way down. You just need to shop around for better deals. You'll end up thanking yourself in the long run.

## Common Money Saving Tips

*1. Around the house:*

a) Install a pre-fabricated water heater blanket to wrap around your hot water heater. Studies have shown that hot water heaters use a lot of energy to reheat the water that's already in the tank. A pre-fabricated water heater blanket will help insulate your tank and conserve energy.

b) Switch to fluorescent lights. Fluorescent lights last up to nine times longer than traditional light bulbs and use about one-third the electricity.

c) Weatherproof your doors and windows. Check for air leaks and seal with foam tape or insulating material. Air leaks will force your heat or air conditioning system to work harder.

d) Perform manufacturer-recommended service on air conditioning and heating systems. Filters often become clogged and system performance suffers.

e) Water your lawn once a week. A healthy lawn only needs one inch of water per week. Anything more than that is excessive. Make sure your lawn is fertilized properly.

f) Install ceiling fans to help circulate air. Heat rises and ceiling fans can help circulate warm air. They're also very effective in the summertime.

*2. While you're shopping:*

a) Use coupons for everyday items. You can often save anywhere from 10 to 50 percent by using coupons.

b) Buy generic when it's appropriate. I know that generic things aren't as cool as the real thing, but they will save you lots of money and serve the same purpose.

c) Comparison shop for big ticket items. Wouldn't you rather save a couple thousand dollars on your new car by driving a little further than giving your local salesman a nice commission?

d) Be wary of bulk purchases. Stores like Costco like to make you think you're getting a great deal by buying in bulk. Sometimes, you'll actually pay more to buy in bulk. Be a savvy shopper!

*3. When dealing with your car insurance:*

a) Keep your deductibles at $500.00. This will save you a bunch of money in the long run. A $1000 deductible is often too much money to come up with on short notice.

b) Don't pay for unneeded coverage. The state minimums for bodily injury and property damage liability are usually sufficient.

c) Check for discounts. Auto insurers have many discounts such as good driver, good student, anti-lock brakes, airbags, and theft deterrent system. Ask your insurer if you qualify for any discounts. Taking a defensive driving class through your department of licensing will earn you an automatic discount.

d) Don't pay for emergency roadside assistance if your vehicle has a valid factory warranty. Most dealers include this option in your factory warranty. You can also use services like AAA to get cheaper emergency roadside assistance. AAA can be reached at **(1-800-562-2582)**.

e) Forget the rental fee. Insurance rental fees usually end up costing you more money over time. How often do you use this service? Pay for car rentals out of pocket. The chances of you getting your money back on this deal are slim to none.

## The Biggest Raise You'll Ever Receive

I decided to save the biggest money-saving tip for last. The biggest raise you will see throughout your lifetime is when you pay off debt. I know there's nothing like pointing out the obvious, but the last statement is so true. When a revolving bill is removed from your monthly obligations, your finances become more flexible. There is nothing more annoying than having no flexibility in your financial life. Well, maybe having only two sheets of toilet paper left on the roll when you're in a big hurry.

When you get into the habit of paying cash, you create a buffer between you and debt. The buffer keeps on getting wider and, eventually, debt will not even become a concern. Imagine having no car payments, mortgage payments, loan payments, or credit card payments. It can be done in a relatively short period of time. When you've achieved this level in your financial organization, your money starts to work for you. You are no longer working for your money.

Becoming debt free is not only good for your financial outlook, but it's also good for your health. Money is one of the major causes of stress. Don't allow yourself to become entangled in a web of debt. Wouldn't you like to put yourself in a position where you never have to make a mortgage payment? That sounds like a recipe for healthy living to me.

## Create Action Plans for Goals

All of us dream about becoming rich or accomplishing major achievements during our lifetime. It's important to know that you'll never accomplish your financial goals unless you take action and create a plan. Only you can customize a plan that works for your lifestyle. If your goal is to get rid of credit card debt, make definitive plans and stick to them. Mary Kay Cosmetics has a very catchy saying to help motivate their sales force that also fits for financial planning: *"Plan your work and work your plan."*

As we discussed in chapter three, saving 10 percent of your income is the golden rule and part of the foundation for wealth creation. Paying down debt is the other part of wealth creation. Both of these rules work together. These two rules should be the focal points of your financial action plans. If you fail to incorporate both of these rules together, you'll end up working harder than a one-legged man in an ass kicking contest to become financially independent. Take pride in your financial organization and create a large debt buffer.

# CHAPTER 5
# DECIPHERING THE FINANCIAL WORLD

Okay, I promise not to bore you too much in this chapter. I'm not going to pump an endless stream of mind-numbing data into your brain. My intent is to give you a basic understanding of how the financial markets work today. It's always dangerous to dive head first into something you don't know anything about. Many people have investments, and they don't understand what they just bought, or if they got a good deal or not. You need to educate yourself about core market fundamentals to be a successful investor.

## A Quick Market Down and Dirty

What is *stock*? Webster defines stock as "the proprietorship element in corporation divided to give the owners an interest and usu." So what the hell does that mean? Even the dictionary tries to complicate the meaning of stock. I just had to look up the word 'usu' because it blew my mind that the dictionary would describe such a simple word in this manner. Supposedly, usu is short for usufruct and is the legal right to use and enjoy the benefits and profits of something belonging to another. To make this easier, let's define stock as a portion of a company that represents ownership.

These portions of the company are called *shares*. So you could hypothetically own 100 shares of Microsoft stock. Companies often issue millions of shares of stock for private or public sale. When you own shares of stock, you become a *shareholder* and actually own a portion of the company. If a company is profitable, your shares of stock increase in value, and if company is unsuccessful, your shares decrease in value.

Companies issue stock because they want to generate income to fund growth. In return, they often pay dividends to gain investor trust and encourage more people to buy their stock. There are two types of stock: *common stock and preferred stock.* Common stock is regular stock, whose price rises and falls with the stock market. Preferred stock is stock with benefits and it normally pays regular dividends. The benefits of preferred stock allow shareholders to have first dibs on assets if the company should go under. Preferred stock is often issued to investors who own a lot of shares, and a large portion of the company. Most stocks are issued as common stock.

Stocks are divided into different categories based on their market value. A company's market value is known as *market capitalization* or *market cap.* Market cap is determined by the stock price multiplied by the number of shares the company has outstanding. Large-cap stocks are those valued at 5 billion dollars or more. Mid-cap stocks are valued between 1 and 5 billion and small-cap stocks are valued at 1 billion or less.

What is the *stock market*? The stock market is a securities exchange where stocks can be bought and sold. When a stock is in high demand, its price rises, and when it is out of favor, the price decreases. The stock market is all about supply and demand.

Stocks are traded through *exchanges.* Exchanges allow investors a centralized place to trade securities. The New York Stock Exchange (NYSE) is the largest place to trade stocks. Other exchanges include the American Stock Exchange and the National Association of Securities Dealers (NASDAQ). The NASDAQ is an electronic exchange that uses a vast array of computers to perform trades.

The stock market is divided into *indexes.* Indexes are designed to give investors an overall gauge of market performance. Most investors track the Dow Jones Industrial Average Index (DOW), the Standard and Poor's 500 Index (S&P 500), and the NASDAQ Composite Index. There are other indexes, but those are the major ones. Investors can measure market performance through indexes by tracking *volume.* Volume is a value of how many stocks were bought and sold in one day. High volume is associated with a lot of trader activity and low volume is associated with little activity.

The *DOW* is the most recognized index. It consists of the 30 largest companies in the United States. The list is periodically changed as new companies emerge and grow larger than other companies on the list. Huge companies such as General Electric and McDonalds make up this list. Even though this index is used as an indication of market health, it's not entirely accurate. Thirty companies aren't a good representation of the market whole. Don't get your panties in a knot when you hear about the DOW dropping 100 points in a day because it doesn't necessarily mean that the market is tanking. Perhaps two or three of the DOW 30 stocks had bad earnings reports that day or something like that.

The *S&P 500* is the most accurate representation of the market as a whole. This index represents the 500 largest U.S. companies. These 500 companies encompass all of the major industry sectors, such as healthcare and finance. The S&P 500 can be thought of as a benchmark to grade performance. You'll often hear people say that they want to beat the market. This means that they want their investments to have a higher return than the S&P 500.

The last index we are going to talk about is the *NASDAQ Composite.* Don't confuse this with the NASDAQ Exchange. The NASDAQ Composite consists mostly of technology companies and internet stocks. This index is unique because many of the companies are at the cutting edge of technology and constantly bringing change to the table. The drawback to this index is that many of the stocks are volatile. This was one of the reasons why there was a technology stock bubble burst in early 2000.

Okay, are you still with me? I know this may be new information for a lot of you, but I promise that I'll bring everything together for you by the end of this book. When I was first learning about the stock market, I liked to think of it like a grocery store. A grocery store runs a lot like the stock market.

The grocery stores themselves are like stock exchanges. Each store is a little different, but they are centralized places where store managers can buy or sell whatever they want. A grocery store chain would be like the NASDAQ because they are linked. The grocery store manager would represent a trader or investor and is trying to turn a profit. The manager buys goods from vendors and then sells them for profit to consumers at fair market value.

The products the store sells represent all the companies in the stock market. All grocery stores are divided into sections, such as produce, meat, dairy, and canned goods. These sections represent the industry sectors of the stock market. A grouping of the store's top selling products would represent an index. This index helps gauge how well the store is doing as a whole. The amount of volume the store is producing is representative of how much the store is buying or selling in a day. All the grocery stores put together would make up the stock market.

**Table 5-1 Grocery Store Market Analogy**

All Grocery Stores → The Stock Market

Individual Stores → Represent Stock Exchanges

Store Managers → Represent Traders and Investors

Store Products → Represent Companies in Market

Store Sections → Represent Industry Sectors

Amount Bought/Sold → Volume

## Da Bulls, Da Bears

Now it's time to talk a little about market trends. You may hear news anchors talking about bulls and bears when referencing the stock market. They're not talking about getting gored in the ass by a 2000 pound beast like Billy Crystal in City Slickers. They're referring to investor confidence. If investors are buying stocks in frenzy, they are said to be *bullish,* and if they're selling stocks rapidly, they are said to be *bearish.*

When stock prices are increasing in an uptrend over several quarters, we are in a *bull market.* When the opposite is true, we are in a *bear market.* Investors often base their investing strategies on bullish or bearish reports. *Value stocks* are regularly sought after during bearish reports. A value stock is a stock that is out-of-favor with stock market analysts. The company may have suffered some lawsuits or had lower than expected earnings reports. Value stocks are often well-managed companies with good fundamentals. Investors try to buy these stocks at a discount from regular prices. *Growth stocks* are small companies bought during times of economic prosperity. Traders like to gamble on whether or not a company will grow and produce large amounts of positive earnings. Growth stocks thrive during bull markets.

## ♫ I Like to Move It, Move It ♫

So how do we know which direction the market is going? It's constantly moving up, down, and sideways. General market health can be determined by *moving averages.* A moving average is the average of a stock or index's closing price over a period of time. A long-term moving average is calculated over a period of 200 days, and a short-term average is over 50 days. When a stock or index closes above its moving average, the trend is positive, or bullish, and when a stock closes below its moving average, the trend is bearish. Stock market health is usually determined by tracking the S&P 500 moving averages. Refer to Table 5-2 on the next page for a sample moving average chart.

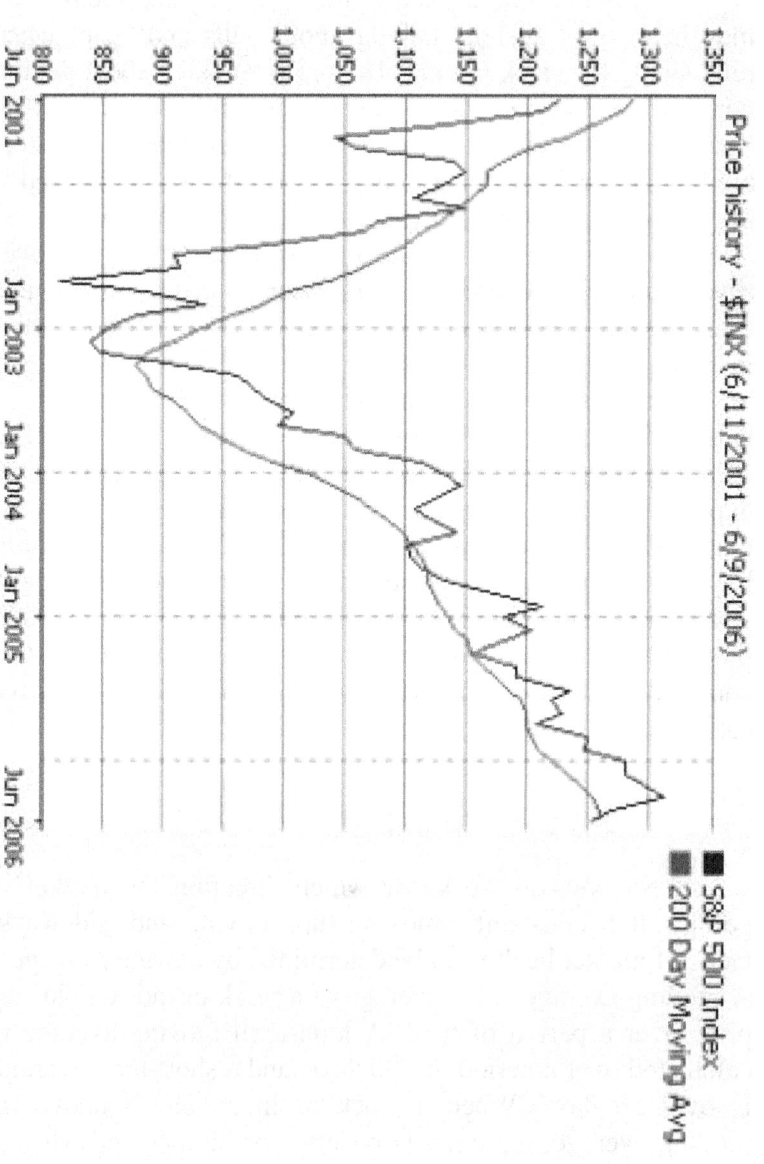


**Table 5-2 S&P 500 Moving Average Chart**

As you can see on the chart above, the 200 day moving average gives a good indication of how the market health was during a five year period starting in June 2001. After the September 11th terrorist attacks in 2001, the market fell significantly lower than the 200 day moving average. The market was in an obvious downtrend and very bearish. Around August of 2003, the market started to rebound and headed above the 200 day moving average. The market was very bullish during that timeframe. You can never predict which direction the market is going to go, but you can definitely tell what the trend is.

Moving averages can be viewed through many sources. I like to use the free service MSN provides on their Money homepage. You can type in whatever stock or index you want to view and customize the views to match exactly what you want to see. MSN can be found on the internet at http://www.msn.com.

## Ticker Symbols

People are often curious about what all the garbage is that is scrolling across the bottom of television screen on CNBC. Those are called *ticker symbols* and they represent individual stocks or indexes. For example, the ticker symbol for Microsoft is MSFT and the S&P 500 Index is represented by ticker symbol $INX. Every stock or index has its own unique ticker symbol. Channels like CNBC scroll active real-time quotes so traders can view individual stock activity. Real-time quotes can be accessed at any time online via brokerage websites or free financial service websites like MSN or Yahoo. Just type a ticker symbol in and click go.

## Trading Lingo

There are some terms you will need to become familiar with when buying stock. It won't be quite as difficult as learning to roll your rrs in high school Spanish class, but the terms can be confusing. Please make sure you understand these terms before buying any stock.

*Market Order:* A market order is an order to buy or sell a security at the current market price.

*Limit Order:* A limit order is an order to buy or sell a security at a specified price. The trade is executed only if the price of the stock has reached or surpassed the level the trader specified.

*Stop-Loss*: An order to sell a security when the price falls to a specified level.

*Stop-Limit Order:* An order to buy or sell a security that combines the features of a stop-loss and limit order. Once the stop-loss price has been reached, a limit order is processed to buy at a specified price.

*Day Orders:* Normal orders to buy or sell a security are known as day orders which mean that the broker can only execute your trade during that specific trading day.

*Good-Til-Cancelled Order:* An order to buy or sell a security at a specific or limit price that lasts until the order is completed or cancelled. These orders can last longer than one trading day.

## Brokerages

You've heard me use the word "brokerages" a couple of times throughout this book, but I have yet to explain what it is. A brokerage is an agency that buys or sells shares of stock via the stock exchanges. They are basically the middleman you have to go through to get shares of stocks. Brokerages hire licensed brokers that perform stock trades on your behalf. Most of the trades are now done electronically. Brokerages will take you to the cleaners if you're not careful. They work off of commissions and charge fees to buy and sell stock.

You have to choose the right broker based on your investment style. There are basically two types of brokers: *full-service* and *deep-discount*. Full-service brokers charge high commission fees, but they also tend to offer more services. They cater to their customers and provide things like detailed technical analysis, individual counseling, and stock tips. An investor with a ton of cash is the type of client a full-service broker seeks out. These types of investors are sometimes called "whales." A deep-discount broker charges low commissions and is generally only concerned about processing your trade. Many young investors open full-service brokerage accounts and are not aware that they are paying way too much money in commissions. An investor just starting out should always opt for a deep-discount brokerage account.

Setting up a brokerage account is essential for your journey to financial freedom. You have to provide yourself an avenue to buy stocks. However, you want to make sure that your broker is reputable and you're comfortable navigating through their website. It's also important that your broker lets you deposit funds either by direct deposit or mail and that they pay you the same way.

I recommend the following deep-discount brokerage services:

1. **TD Ameritrade** (http://www.tdameritrade.com)
    a) $9.99 Market and Limit Order trades.
    b) No quarterly or annual maintenance fees.
    c) 24/7 customer support.
2. **ShareBuilder** (http://www.sharebuilder.com)
    a) $4.00 Automatic Investments.
    b) No minimum value to open account.
    c) No annual maintenance fees.
3. **Scottrade** (http://www.scottrade.com)
    a) $7.00 market and limit order trades.
    b) Free streaming news from Dow Jones.
    c) No accounts fees or transfer fees.

4. **Your Credit Union**
    a) Umbrella your accounts as you see fit.
    b) Look for credit unions affiliated with CUNA Mutual Group. They provide excellent brokerage options through your hometown credit union.
    c) Check out http://www.cunamutual.com to find a credit union associated with CUNA Mutual.

## Technical Analysis

Ouch! This subtitle doesn't sound so pleasant, does it? We're not going to get too involved in this stuff because it's not really necessary. On the contrary, you do need to be aware of a few figures because they relate directly to successful stock picking. You'll never have to worry about computing most of these numbers by yourself because there are tons of websites like MSN and Yahoo who compute the numbers for you. These figures are listed under a company's financials. I want you to be aware of how the important figures are generated so that you have a better understanding of what they mean.

*EPS:* Stands for earnings per share and is a company's net income divided by the common shares outstanding. EPS shows how profitable a company is.

*P/E Ratio*: Stands for price to earnings ratio and is computed by dividing the stock price by earnings per share. A company's P/E ratio should be about half, or less than half of the earnings growth. If a company has an EPS growth rate of 29 percent, their P/E ratio should be around 15 to 20. Investors will often pay more for a stock than it's worth because they are anticipating higher growth rates. It's always risky to pay a premium for stocks.

*ROE:* Stands for return on equity and is figured by taking the company's net worth and dividing it by the difference between a company's assets and liabilities. An ROE above 20 percent is excellent.

*P/S Ratio:* Stands for price-to-sales ratio. Figure this by dividing the current stock price by the sales per share. Good stocks have low P/S ratios. A good P/S ratio is 1.0 or less.

*Beta:* Beta is a measure of a stock's volatility compared to the overall market. Stocks are compared to the S&P 500 index, and a beta of 1.0 or less is considered low volatility compared to the overall market. A beta higher than 1.0 indicates high volatility compared to the overall market.

*Debt-to-Equity Ratio:* This number is equal to a company's long-term debt divided by the common shareholders' equity. If a company has long-term debt of $5000 and shareholders' equity of $15,000, then their debt-to-equity ratio would equal .33. If a company has a ratio greater than 1, their assets are financed primarily through debt. A ratio of less than one is excellent. A stock with little or no debt is outstanding.

*P/B Value*: Stands for price-to-book value and is computed by taking a company's market capitalization value and dividing it by its book value. Book value is how much a company is worth on paper if you added up all its assets and subtracted their liabilities. A high price-to-book value suggests that the market may be overvalued and a low price-to-book value suggests that the market may be undervalued. This figure indicates what a company is worth, should it go bankrupt and become liquidated.

*PEG Ratio:* A stock's price-to-earnings ratio divided by its yearly growth rate. This number determines what an investor pays for each unit of growth. A company with a P/E ratio of 10 and a yearly growth rate of 20 percent has a PEG ratio of .5. A stock with a PEG between 1.2 and 1.5 is considered excellent.

*Acid Test:* This test is figured by subtracting the company's inventories from the current assets and dividing that number by the current liabilities. A company must have a one-to-one ratio to the pass the test. For every $1 of debt, the company has $1 of current assets minus inventories. This value must be greater than one.

So, do you see which kind of stocks we are looking for? We are seeking stocks with solid financials. We want stocks with low debt-to-equity ratios and high return-on-equity ratios. Good stocks have a 1.0 or lower price-to-sales ratio, low P/E ratios in comparison to growth, and a beta of 1.0 or less. The stock should have a PEG between 1.2 and 1.5, and a low price-to-book value. Finally, a good stock should pass the Acid Test.

## Mutual Funds

For all of you who are sighing and complaining about learning technical analysis, I have some good news. Normally, I would ask somebody if they wanted some cheese and crackers to go with that whine, but I'll refrain this time. Mutual funds are professionally managed companies that bring together money from many people and invest in stocks, bonds, or other assets. So, if you don't feel like picking your own stocks, you can let a professional do it for you.

There are many different mutual funds that suit every type of investor's needs. It's estimated that there are over 10,000 mutual funds just in North America. Some funds focus on aggressive growth, others try to match the S&P 500 or other index benchmarks, and some focus on individual sectors. Mutual funds are easy to invest in and give investors many options. The options cater to every investing style and individual investor risk tolerance level. We will discuss how to pick the right mutual funds in chapter seven.

There are definitely some advantages to investing in mutual funds, but there are a few disadvantages. The advantages are that your funds are professionally managed and you don't have to worry about any technical analysis. The disadvantages are that you don't have any control over what the fund invests in, and you pay higher fees than if you picked your own stocks.

Some people like to be in the driver's seat with their investment money. They want absolute control over where their money is going. Other people would rather have somebody do all the work for them and reap the rewards of stock ownership. It's worth it for some people to pay extra management fees to invest in mutual funds. Mutual funds are designed for investors who don't want to spend a lot of time scouring over their investments every month.

Now we need to discuss what types of mutual funds to avoid. Some funds charge you a lot of extra fees and you aren't getting anything back in return for those fees. Studies have proven that loaded funds have no advantage over no-load funds. Avoid loaded funds! A loaded fund makes you pay sales charges when buying or selling shares. This fee can range anywhere from three to eight percent of the full transaction. It makes no sense to invest in loaded funds. Always invest in *no-load mutual funds.*

A good mutual fund should have an *expense ratio* of no more than 1.5 percent. An expense ratio is what a fund charges you to invest with them. These fees include management fees, 12B-1 fees, and other expenses, such as administration fees. *12B-1* fees are usually brokerage commission fees and advertising fees. Don't let yourself get burned on 12B-1 fees. Your portfolio will suffer while the mutual fund manager is sipping margaritas at Jimmy Buffet's Margaritaville restaurant on your behalf.

You can open an account directly through mutual fund companies instead of opening a brokerage account if you choose to do so. I do both. I want my retirement investment money to go into a well-run mutual fund, and my other investment money to go to my own brokerage account where I can make all the calls. I like some control, but not 100 percent control. I feel better knowing that my retirement money is being managed by a professional. We'll discuss portfolio setup in detail in chapter eight.

Here is a list of mutual fund companies that I recommend:

**Vanguard: 1-877-662-7447**
**http://www.vanguard.com**

**Transamerica: 1-800-891-7587**
**http://www.transamericafunds.com**

**Fidelity: 1-800-343-3548**
**http://www.fidelity.com**

## Exchange Traded Funds (ETF's)/ Index Funds

There are many derivatives of mutual funds and they are all designed to make life easier for you. We are such a fast-paced society and we are constantly creating shortcuts to make our lives easier. We don't like to spend extra time on our finances, so we have created ways to invest our money in investment vehicles, like mutual funds, with the same convenience as regular stocks. Regular stocks are easy to buy and sell, while traditional mutual funds require more interaction to buy or sell. You usually have to contact a customer service representative to sell mutual fund shares. An *ETF fund* is a fund that tracks indexes, but trades like a stock. The fund consists of all the stocks that make up an index. They are extremely easy to buy and sell and you can purchase them through your brokerage account.

Sometimes you will hear ETF's called *Index Funds.* Don't get confused if you log on to your brokerage account to search for ETF funds and you see index funds in the same section. The only difference is that mutual funds often have index funds in their fund family, but won't offer ETF's. ETF's are generally traded through brokerages only. They are basically the same thing as Index Funds though.

An example of an ETF fund would be the NASDAQ 100 Trust (ticker symbol QQQQ). This ETF tracks the top

100 companies in the NASDAQ composite index. The expense ratios are usually very low with ETF's. Owning shares of an ETF through your brokerage account will save you a lot of time and money. You'll finally have time to wax your back hair instead of waiting on hold with customer service at your regular mutual fund company. Here is a list of popular ETF funds that I recommend:

**S&P 500 Index SPDR: S&P 500 Deposits and Receipt**
Ticker Symbol- (SPY)

**DIA Trust 1: Dow Jones Industrial Average Trust 1**
Ticker Symbol- (DIA)

**NASDAQ 100 Trust 1: NASDAQ Composite Index**
Ticker Symbol- (QQQQ)

## Prime Rate—The Little Engine that Could

The driving force behind the economy is a powerful little engine called the *prime rate.* The prime rate is the interest rate that banks charge to customers with a high degree of creditworthiness. Major companies or corporations would be examples of customers with a high degree of credit worthiness. The economy lives and breathes off of the current prime rate. The stock market will flinch on a rumor that the prime interest rate is about to rise or fall. It's like seeing a redheaded step-child duck for cover when an upset parent threatens a violent backhanded slap.

The Federal Reserve is responsible for maintaining the prime rate. They raise and lower it based on the economic indications of *inflation* or *deflation.* Inflation is the general upward price movement of goods or services in the economy. Deflation is the opposite of inflation and is the general downward price movement of goods or services in the economy. The U.S. economy has an average inflationary rate of two to three percent a year. This is important to you as an investor because the purchasing power of your money decreases every single year. Deflation is very rare and you shouldn't count on it to occur. Damn, it would be nice if it would happen a little more often though!

The prime rate helps us determine where we should be investing the bulk of our money. When the prime rate is being lowered, the Federal Reserve is trying to jumpstart the economy. When the prime rate is being raised, the Federal Reserve is trying to slow the economy. This information is a treasure map for investors because it tells us exactly where our money needs to be to gain the best returns. Please pay close attention to Table 5-3 below because it will make you rich if you invest with this type of style.

**TABLE 5-3**
**PRIME RATE INVESTMENT CHART**

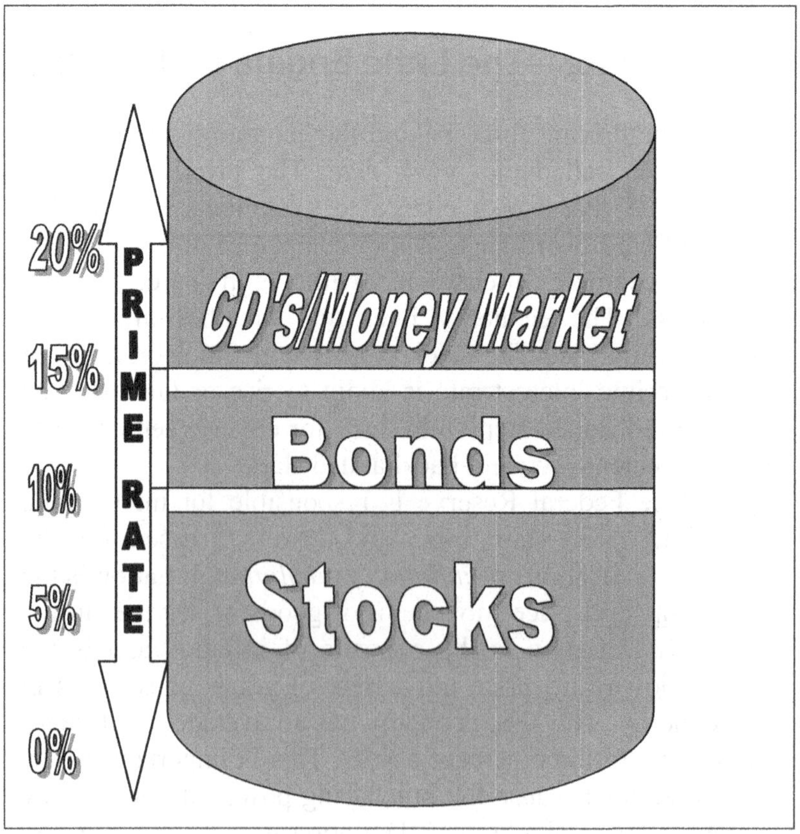

As you can see from the chart above, the prime rate lays a roadmap for our investment strategy. When the prime rate is below nine percent, we want to be heavily invested in stocks because the economy is booming and the stock market is giving investors high returns. When the prime rate climbs higher than nine percent, we want to focus on bonds because they are more stable than stocks. If inflation is running rampant like it did in the late 1970s and early 1980s, we need to put our money into high-interest cash accounts like CDs and money markets. During the early 1980s, CDs and money markets were returning at rates as high as 17 percent. When situations like that happen, we need to jump all over them as investors. We will discuss portfolio diversification based on prime rate in detail in chapter eight. The current prime rate can be viewed at http://www.primerate.net.

## Financial Data in a Nutshell

We finally made it to the end of this chapter and it's kind of ironic that I can sum it up in a few sentences. This is the stuff that people don't like to learn. You have to have a very basic understanding of how the markets flow to be a successful investor. We must pay attention to the prime rate and react accordingly. A good investor buys individual stocks that pass our technical analysis, stock mutual funds, or ETF's/index funds with low expense ratios when the prime rate is below nine percent. Additionally, successful investors shift their money to bond funds or individual bonds when the prime rate is above nine percent. Finally, a smart trader dumps the majority of their investments into CDs or money markets when the prime rate is surging over 14 percent.

Alright, I think it's break time and it's definitely beer-thirty! In the coming chapter, we are going to discuss specific investments that will give you the best bang for your buck. So, take a break and come back ready to take some notes!

# CHAPTER 6
# BENEFICIAL INVESTMENTS FOR YOU!

We are at the point of the book where we need to bust out our financial journey roadmap to see where we are. Things are still kind of scattered and we need to start tailoring a plan for our investment money. We've learned all about financial suicide, debt, and how to get out of debt. We also talked about the golden rule, financial organization, and got a basic understanding of financial markets. Now we can focus on specific investments that will fatten your wallet or designer purse.

All of us already know that there are two different categories in our portfolio. The first category is savings and we are aware that it's broken down into three parts: an emergency fund, short-term savings fund, and a long-term savings fund. The second category is the investment side of our portfolio. The investment portion of our portfolio consists of one or more retirement accounts and a non-retirement account. Remember that we're looking for long-term growth out of our investments and we're not interested in the short-term. The money in the investment portion of the portfolio is not to be spent until it has had a chance to compound and grow. The savings portion of our portfolio covers the short-term.

## Allocating Portfolio Income

There has to be a balance between the savings and investment sides of our portfolio. The savings side is your number one priority when starting out. Once your emergency account is fully funded, and your short-term and long-term savings are established, you can shift your focus from the savings category to the investment side. Don't forget that your short-term and long-term savings need regular contributions! Now a portion of your mandatory 10 percent savings from your income will go towards your savings category, and the rest will go towards the investment side.

You've effectively put yourself in a position of leverage. You're able to cover any unforeseen emergencies and pay cash for large ticket items beyond your budget, while simultaneously investing your money for long-term growth. I'd say your finances are looking pretty sexy at this point. Maybe a 70-year old man in a leopard thong is sexier, but you get my point. You are cruising down the road at a nice pace to financial freedom when you reach this plateau. This stage doesn't happen overnight, but it can be accomplished in a relatively short period of time if you're motivated enough.

## Start your Roth IRA Retirement Account

Many people can't fathom the fact that they should start saving for retirement in their 20s. It doesn't occur to people that this should even be a priority because retirement is still decades away. The reality is that retirement is an expensive undertaking. To maintain a productive lifestyle into our 80s or 90s, we need a lot of money to support this. Healthcare costs are significant during our later years. I don't know about you, but I don't want to be looking under the couch cushions for change to buy my Depends undergarments when I'm 80 years old.

Uncle Sam was kind enough to allow us to invest for our retirement without paying taxes on the growth. This type of account is called a *Roth IRA*. Roth IRA stands for individual retirement account and provides tax-free growth. This is a huge benefit to you! Tax free growth will save you bucko bucks in the long run. There are yearly contribution limits and the money cannot be withdrawn until you're 59½ years old unless you pay a penalty or use the money for a mortgage down payment. Never withdraw money from your retirement plan during the penalty phase! There are also income restrictions associated with Roth IRAs. People who earn over $95,000 a year or $150,000 as a couple cannot contribute to Roth IRAs. The contribution limits for Roth IRAs are listed in Table 6-1 below.

**Roth IRA Contribution Limits Table 6-1**

| Yr. | Below 49 Yrs Old | Above 50 Yrs Old |
|---|---|---|
| 2006 | $4,000 | $5,000 |
| 2007 | $4,000 | $5,000 |
| 2008 | $5,000 | $6,000 |

A person cannot contribute more than the limit in a given tax year. Tax years are from April 16th to April 15th of the following year. The Federal Reserve will raise the contribution limits over time by $500 increments based on the degree of inflation.

The great part about Roth IRAs is that they can be invested in almost anything you want. I highly recommend investing in an S&P 500 index fund or a *balanced mutual fund*. You want to invest in something that is going to grow steadily over time and be less volatile during bear markets. A balanced mutual fund is great for a Roth IRA because it blends stocks, bonds, and cash. Sound familiar? A balanced fund offers returns, no matter how the prime rate is fluctuating. When the prime rate is high, bonds and cash accounts perform well, and when the prime rate is low, stocks perform well. A good balanced fund will consist of about 60 to 70 percent stocks and 30 to 40 percent bonds and cash.

A Roth IRA can be opened through any mutual fund company or brokerage. It's absolutely imperative that you open a Roth IRA for your retirement account. So here's a tip for your Roth IRA: *sink every investment dollar you have available into your Roth IRA account until you reach the contribution limit.*

## 401K or SEP Retirement Plans

Another option some of you may have available is to participate in your employer's 401K or Simplified Employee Pension (SEP) retirement plans. This plan isn't available to all of us, but you should definitely take advantage of it if your employer offers it. Much like a Roth IRA, a 401K grows tax-free, since the taxes are deferred until the money is withdrawn. Many companies will match a portion of your contributions to help your retirement account grow. This is free money!

Most companies allow you to invest in their stock or a variety of mutual funds. Be careful not to put all your eggs in one basket! Many people have their entire retirement accounts hinging on the success of their company's stock. That is a dangerous undertaking and not recommended. Don't get caught with your pants down like many Enron employees did. Pick the most diversified fund with the lowest expense ratio.

There are a couple of drawbacks to 401Ks. First of all, you have limited options on where your money can be invested. Your employer will usually pick one mutual fund family. What if those mutual funds are loaded funds and have very high expense ratios? We have to be realistic here though. If your employer is going to match your contributions, it's worth it to pay higher fees because you're essentially getting free money. Contact your human resources department to get more information about your company's 401K retirement plan.

Just like a Roth IRA, you want to max out your yearly contributions. A 401K has a limit of $15,000 per year in 2006. This number will be adjusted for inflation in $500 increments the same way a Roth IRA is. So, if your employee offers a 401K or SEP, forget about a Roth IRA and focus on contributing to this retirement account until you're able to contribute the maximum yearly contribution.

The savviest of all investors max out their 401K contributions and then open a Roth IRA to do the same. This is a brilliant plan because these people are double-dipping. They are simultaneously growing two tax deferred retirement accounts. However, that is a lot of money to save. It's not unrealistic though. Let's say that you and your significant other have a combined yearly income of $160,000. Saving only 10 percent of your annual income would be enough to max out the yearly contributions for a 401K and Roth IRA. I guarantee you that you will retire a millionaire if you max out your retirement plan yearly contributions. Remember that most millionaires save 15 to 20 percent of their take-home pay.

## Dollar-Cost Averaging

How do we come up with a manageable way to deposit funds into our retirement accounts while focusing on contributing the maximum limit? That's simple. We *dollar-cost average* our available monthly investment income. Dollar-cost averaging means that you invest the same amount of money of every month towards your retirement accounts.

Let's say that you have $300 a month to dump into your portfolio. $100 is going to go toward your short-term and long-term savings accounts and the remaining $200 is going to go towards your Roth IRA or 401K retirement account. That $200 is going to buy a different amount of shares each month. More shares will be purchased when the price of the mutual fund is lower, and fewer will be bought when the price is higher. This is more effective than lump sum investing. *Lump sum investing* is when you buy a large amount of stock and pay for it all at once instead of over time. Dollar-cost averaging allows you to buy shares for an average price instead of paying what the market dictates. Over time, a dollar-cost investor will make more money than a lump sum investor.

The idea is to dollar-cost average the same amount of money every month until your monthly investment income increases. When your investment income increases, you want to dollar-cost average the new amount. Refer to Table 6-2 below for a dollar-cost averaging example.

**Sally's Dollar-Cost Averaging Plan Table 6-2**

| Mon | Stk Price | Amt Invested | Shares Bought |
|---|---|---|---|
| Jan. | $39.00 | $200.00 | 5.13 |
| Feb. | $37.25 | $200.00 | 5.37 |
| Mar. | $37.10 | $200.00 | 5.39 |
| Apr. | $38.75 | $200.00 | 5.16 |
| May. | $39.53 | $200.00 | 5.05 |
| Jun. | $41.28 | $200.00 | 4.85 |
| Jul. | $40.12 | $200.00 | 4.99 |
| Aug. | $36.52 | $200.00 | 5.48 |
| Sep. | $38.61 | $200.00 | 5.18 |
| Oct. | $39.98 | $200.00 | 5.00 |
| Nov. | $42.11 | $200.00 | 4.74 |
| Dec. | $41.28 | $200.00 | 4.84 |

**Total Amt Invested** = $2400

**Total Shares Bought** = 61.18

**Avg. Price Paid Per Share** = $39.29

**Avg. Shares Bought** = 5.09

**Lump Sum Investor invests $2400 on June 1st**

**Shares Bought** = 58.14 (3 fewer shares than Sally)

**Price Paid Per Share** = $41.28 ($1.99 more)

As you can see on Table 6-2 above, dollar-cost averaging is an effective way to buy stocks without paying price premiums. Obviously, the lump sum investor would have made more money if they would have bought at the market low in August. But it's nearly impossible to time the market with any consistency. The dollar-cost average investor will always win out in the long run.

## Create a CD Ladder

A great way to maximize the cash in your portfolio is to build a *CD ladder.* A CD ladder is an investment strategy that staggers your CD purchases in such a way in which you can maximize the returns. A CD ladder gives you the flexibility to have CDs mature every year instead of locking in for a long-term rate with a large sum of cash. The goal is to have a five-year CD maturing after five years and every year thereafter. This is an excellent way to save money for long-term savings, or when the investment side of your portfolio is calling for cash. Here are the directions for building a five-year CD with a hypothetical $5,000 investment and $1,000 CDs:

*Step 1: Make Initial Investment*

- *a) Buy three 1-year CDs = $3,000*
- *b) Buy one 2-year CD = $1,000*
- *c) Buy one 5-year CD = $1,000*

*Step 2: End of 1$^{st}$ Year*

- *a) Buy one new 1-year CD with maturing $1,000*
- *b) Buy one new 2-year CD with maturing $1,000*
- *c) Buy one new 5-year CD with maturing $1,000*

*Step 3: End of 2$^{nd}$ Year*

- *a) Replace the maturing 1-year CD with 2-year CD*
- *b) Replace the maturing 2-year CD with 5-year CD*

*Step 4: End of 3$^{rd}$ Year*

- *a) Replace the maturing 2-year CD with 5-year CD*

*Step 5: End of 4th Year*

*a) Replace the maturing 2-year CD with 5-year CD*

*Step 6: End of 5th Year*

*a) Replace the maturing 5-year CD with 5-year CD*

*b) Continue buying 5-year CD every year there after*

## Posting Bond

We've talked a little bit about bonds, but we haven't touched on where you can purchase U.S. savings bonds or treasury bills. The long-term savings account part of your portfolio needs to be posting bond, as I like to call it. Soon, you'll be like Dog the Bounty Hunter with your long blonde mullet and parachute pants, ensuring your savings portfolio is properly bonded.

To set up an account to purchase U.S. government securities, go to http://www.treasurydirect.gov. I highly recommend buying *I-Bonds*. I-Bonds are inflation indexed bonds and are guaranteed to pay higher interest than the current inflationary rate. They are an excellent way to save money without losing money due to inflation. I-Bonds can be bought in the following denominations: $50, $75, $100, $200, $500, $1,000, $5,000, and $10,000. The maximum amount you can purchase in a calendar year is $30,000.

I-bonds can be purchased electronically and take one year to mature, but carry a three-month interest penalty if you cash them in before five years. They can earn interest for up to 30 years if you don't cash them in.

You should only be buying I-bonds for the savings portion of your portfolio. Stick with a bond mutual fund or balanced fund for the investment side of your portfolio. I-bonds aren't intended to be used for timeframes longer than five years unless you want a guaranteed sum of money at a certain time. Stocks will always outperform bonds in the long-term.

## Beneficial Investments Summary

After reading this section, you should be fully focused on funding the savings portion of your portfolio and putting all the leftover money into the investment side of your portfolio starting with a retirement account. Continue funding your Roth IRA or 401K by dollar-cost averaging until you've contributed the maximum yearly amount. Finally, build a CD ladder and invest in I-bonds to fund your long-term savings account. Please refer to Table 6-3 for portfolio organization.

**Table 6-3 Portfolio Organization**

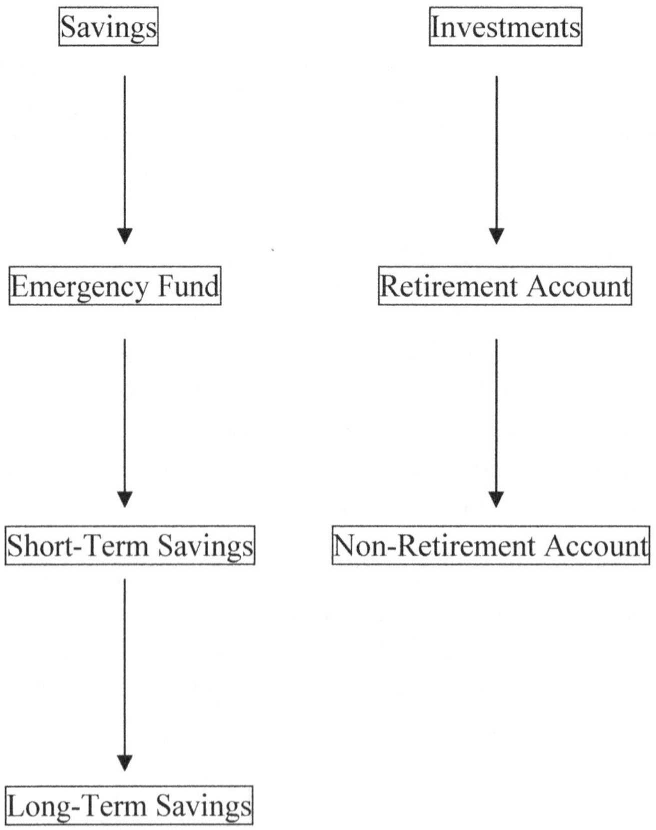

| Table 6-4 Investment Organization | | |
|---|---|---|
| **Account Type** | **Amount** | **Where to Put Money** |
| Roth IRA | *Yearly Max | Index Fund or Balanced Fund |
| 401 K | *Yearly Max | Broadest fund w/t low expense |
| Non-Retire | Any $ Left | Mutual Funds/ Individual Stock |

# CHAPTER 7
# EDUCATED DECISION-MAKING

This chapter is dedicated to those individuals who want to be in the driver's seat and have full control of their investments. You don't have to have a degree in economics to make the right stock selections, but your hamster wheel in your brain has to spin a little bit. Investors who decide to build their own personal mutual fund have the chance to create a much larger portfolio than a regular mutual fund investor. The fees are significantly lower when you choose your own stocks. Management and administrative fees become null and void. I applaud those of you with the entrepreneurial spirits who are motivated to pick stocks.

We've already established that we are looking for stocks that meet certain criteria. Stocks need to be screened for healthiness by using a stock screening guide. The guide helps us ensure that we are checking all the signs that make up a healthy stock. All of the stocks contained in your portfolio must pass the stock screening test to remain on your team. Sorry, we're cutting the stocks that don't make the cut just like a basketball coach who cuts the tall white kid who can't dunk. We always want strong performers with excellent fundamentals representing our portfolio. We're not going to jump in and out of trades at a rapid pace either. It doesn't make any sense to pay extra trade commission fees.

All of us must learn when to buy and sell if we are actively managing our own investment portfolio. Peter Lynch, who is the one of the most successful investors of all-time, often talks about people who become married to stocks. They fall in love with the company and refuse to sell the stock when the fundamentals go down the crapper. It's imperative that you sell a stock when your reason for selling worksheet tells you to.

Throughout this chapter, we will learn how to use a stock screening guide to find winning stocks to buy. Additionally, we will learn how to use a buy and sell worksheet and practice the entire process with actual stocks.

## Stock Screening Guide Part 1 of 2

**Date: ________ Company Name: _____________**

**Ticker: ______ Market Cap: _________**

**Current Price: ______ 52 Week HI: ______ LO: _____**

**P/E Ratio: _______ ROE: _______ P/B Value: ______**

**Acid Test: _______ PEG: _______ P/S Ratio: _______**

**EPS: _____ (Pos/Neg) Net Income Growth Rate: _______**

**Debt-to-Equity Ratio: __________ Beta: ________**

**Stock Price & 200 Day Moving Avg: ________ (↑, ↓, →)**

**Insider Trading: ________ (More Buying/More Selling)**

**Stock Buyback: _________ (Yes/No)**

**Intrinsic Value: _______ (Yes/No)**

**Stock Screening Guide Part 2 of 2**

1) Is the P/E ratio near or less than half of the net income growth rate? Yes________ No________

2) Is the ROE greater than 20 percent? Yes____ No____

3) Is the P/B value less than the average of other companies in the same industry? Yes____ No____

4) Does the stock pass the Acid Test? Yes____ No____

5) Does the stock have a PEG less than 2? Yes___ No___

6) Is the P/S Ratio less than 1? Yes____ No____

7) Is the EPS positive? Yes_____ No_____

8) Is the net income growth rate above 15 percent?

Yes______ No______

9) Is the debt-to-equity ratio .25 or less? Yes___ No___

10) Is the beta less than 1.0? Yes____ No____

11) Is the stock price above the 200 day moving average?
Yes_____ No_____

12) Are insiders buying more than selling? Yes___ No__

13) Is the company buying back stock? Yes____ No___

14) Does the company have intrinsic value?

Yes_____ No_____

15) Passes Screening = Answering Yes 12 or more times
Fails Screening = Answering No more than 3 times
Pass________ Fail_______

As you can see, the stock screening guide lists a series of data that you must answer when screening potential stocks to add to your investment portfolio. The stock screening guide's job is to weed out any stocks that don't match our criteria for a successful growth stock. Growth stocks are the momentum-makers for our portfolio.

Start by finding a stock to screen and begin filling out the information on the top of the sheet. Log onto the internet and go to a financial service website like MSN Money. Type in the company's ticker symbol and go to their company report or snapshot section. You will find basic data like the P/E Ratio, beta, and market cap value along with the current pricing and 52-week high and low here. A *52-week high and low* are the highest and lowest stock price value during a 52-week period. The debt-to-equity ratio is also listed in the company report section.

The next step is to go to the financial results section and click on the financial highlights tab to view the ROE, EPS, and debt-to-equity ratio. After writing down that data on your sheet, move to the key ratios tab under financial results. You will find the P/B value and P/S ratios in the price ratios section. Continue on to the growth rates tab under "key ratios" to find the net income growth rate. Calculate the Acid Test results and PEG because those values are typically not listed on most financial service websites. Refer to chapter 5 for a refresher on how to calculate the Acid Test and PEG.

To examine the current stock price compared to the 200-day moving average, you must click on the charts tab. Customize the chart to view at least one year of stock prices along with the 200-day moving average. Check to see if the current stock price is positive, negative, or flat in relation to the 200-day moving average.

Insider trading can be viewed by clicking on the insider trading tab. *Insider trading* is trading done by company executives. The trades must be filed to the Securities and Exchange Commission (SEC) so investors can view insider activity. Would you want to buy a stock that all the insiders are selling? That doesn't show investors much faith in the success of their company. Something is fishy when a CEO or somebody on the board of directors sells a large stake of their company stock and continues to promote it to investors. Actions speak louder than words!

Determining whether or not a company participates in a stock buyback program can be a little more difficult to find. You will often have to search the key developments or recent news sections. I've even called the investor relations department of a company to ask them before. Companies that buy back their own shares of stock are confident in their company's future earnings potential.

The last thing you need to fill out on part one of the stock screening guide is whether or not a company has *intrinsic value*. Intrinsic value is the true value of a stock that is not necessarily indicated in the market price. Intrinsic value can be a number one selling brand name, trademarks, copyrights, patents, or a service that no other company can provide or match. Intrinsic value is what makes a company unique and profitable.

Warren Buffett buys stocks that have intrinsic value and great fundamentals. Anheuser-Busch, who makes Budweiser beer, is an example of a company with intrinsic value. They have number one name brand recognition along with a patented beer recipe. They don't call them the King of Beers for nothing! Most people only think of Budweiser for the beer goggles effect or Clydesdales, but this company is a perfect example of intrinsic value that far out weighs their market price on Wall Street.

Intrinsic value is very misunderstood by the majority of investors. Stock market analysts don't understand why super investors like Warren Buffet buy stocks that may be unpopular or out-of-favor. He buys them because they have value way beyond the numbers posted on their financial sheets. Companies that have intrinsic value are the leaders in their industry and their effect can be regional, national, or worldwide.

Part two of the stock screening guide is the question and answer portion of the screening. We are answering specific questions about the data in part one. The data is tailored in such a way that only the best quality stocks survive the test. We don't want mediocre or underperforming stocks in our portfolio. They will drag your portfolio down and eat up any returns your other stocks made.

To pass the screening test, you must answer "yes" to twelve of the questions. To fail the screening test, you must answer "no" to three or more questions. It's extremely difficult to find stocks that pass every section of the screening test. There are a few out there now and again, but it's normally unrealistic to find those stocks. That is why we leave a two question margin of error.

A company may have great fundamentals, but they may not be buying back stock because they are focusing on other ventures. Other companies may meet all the criteria of a good growth stock, but may be below their 200-day moving average because of bearish market conditions. You have to weigh the good against the bad. We will help sort those problems out with the buying and selling worksheet.

Just because a company passes our screening test doesn't mean we are going to automatically bet the farm on the stock. It simply means that we have found a potential addition to our portfolio. I've devised a buying and selling worksheet that will help you decide if we can purchase a stock, or if we need to sell it. Every time we buy or sell a stock, we need to run it through our buying and selling worksheet. It's like a checks and balance system.

The buying and selling worksheet tells us whether or not buying or selling is beneficial to our portfolio. We don't want to own a stock from an industry sector that requires constant innovation to stay successful. Our portfolio needs to consist of stocks that can be expected to perform without developing cutting-edge technology or new products. A great company provides products or services that are always in demand with consumers, vice being trendy at the moment.

## Buying and Selling Worksheet Part 1 of 2

**Buying Questions:**

**1) Is the prime rate currently below 9%? Yes____ No___**

**2) Does the stock pass the screening test? Yes____ No___**

**3) Is the company in a non-competitive industry sector that doesn't require constant innovation to remain successful?**
**Yes_____ No_____**

**4) Does the company have significant intrinsic value?**
**Yes_____ No_____**

**5) Is the stock selling at a discount to earnings?**
**Yes____ No____**

**6) Do the company strengths outweigh the weaknesses?**
**Yes_____ No_____**

**Company Strengths:** ______________________________

______________________________

______________________________

**Company Weakness:** ______________________________

______________________________

______________________________

**7) Buy stock if you answer yes to all the questions. Don't buy stock if you answer no to any question.**

**Investor Decision: Buy_____ Not Buying_____**

## Buying and Selling Worksheet Part 2 of 2

**Selling Questions:**

1) **Is the prime rate currently above 9%? Yes___ No___**

2) **Does the stock fail the screening test? Yes___ No___**

3) **Is the company's growth rate significantly slowing?**
**Yes_____ No_____**

4) **Is the company losing its market appeal?**
**Yes_____ No_____**

5) **Is the company taking on more debt every year?**
**Yes_____ No_____**

6) **Do the company weaknesses outweigh the strengths?**
**Yes_____ No_____**

**Company Strengths: ______________________________**

**______________________________**

**______________________________**

**Company Weakness: ______________________________**

**______________________________**

**______________________________**

7) **Sell if you answer yes to any of the questions.**
**Don't sell if you answer no to all of the questions.**

**Investor Decision: Sell______ Don't Sell_______**

The buying and selling worksheets give you the tools to help make an educated decision on whether or not to buy or sell a stock. The worksheets will help keep you from getting burned on stock selection. A stock can look great on the screening guide, but won't fit the bill for purchasing. The market conditions must also be acceptable and the company has to have staying power.

Britney Spears is a perfect example of a stock that looks good on paper because she was trendy. She is a musical artist who had a lot of success in the beginning of her career due to her sex appeal, but has slowly started to fade away because she really isn't that musically talented. We want to buy the Rolling Stones of stocks. They have lasting intrinsic value, unlike Britney Spears. Their music will still be sought after long after their gone.

We are trying to avoid technology-driven stocks in our portfolio because they cannot be counted on to perform well years down the road. Microsoft was the leader of the pack for years, but has recently been suffering because other companies are developing better search engines and computer-related devices. It's risky to own stock in a company that may not have the same amount of market share 10 years from now. Technology companies are under extreme pressure to develop new products and their products are only popular for short periods of time. Do you think that somebody will develop a better iPod device than Apple Computer's in the next couple of years? I'd bet on it!

Our portfolio should consist of stocks that have significant market share, like Starbucks, Coke, Walgreens and Gillette. These companies have minimal competition because their products or business models are proven. Who is going to compete with Starbucks? People instantly think of them when they are craving a double-caramel latte with extra whipped cream. Companies like this aren't under as much intense pressure as companies like Google or IBM. We've touched a lot on intrinsic value because it's so important to find the companies that have it. Find these companies and buy them when they are not selling for a premium.

## Stock Screening Guide Completed Sample Page 1

**Date:** June 24, 2006 **Company Name:** Alon Energy

**Ticker:** ALJ **Market Cap:** 1.32 B/Mid Cap

**Current Price:** $28.27 **52 Week HI:** $36.20 **LO:** $17.05

**P/E Ratio:** 8.93 **ROE:** 66.44 **P/B Value:** 4.24

**Acid Test:** 1.89 **PEG:** 1.05 **P/S Ratio:** .53

**EPS:** 3.15 **(Pos/Neg) Net Income Growth Rate:** 44.68

**Debt-to-Equity Ratio:** .10 **Beta:** 0

**Stock Price & 200 Day Moving Avg:** ↑ **(↑, ↓, →)**

**Insider Trading:** Buying **(More Buying/More Selling)**

**Stock Buyback:** No **(Yes/No)**

**Intrinsic Value:** Yes **(Yes/No)**

## Stock Screening Guide Completed Sample Page 2

**1) Is the P/E ratio near or less than half of the net income growth rate? Yes _X_ No ___**

**2) Is the ROE greater than 20 percent? Yes _X_ No ___**

**3) Is the P/B value less than the average of other companies in the same industry? Yes ___ No _X_**

**4) Does the stock pass the Acid Test? Yes _X_ No ___**

**5) Does the stock have a PEG less than 2? Yes _X_ No ___**

**6) Is the P/S Ratio less than 1? Yes _X_ No ___**

**7) Is the EPS positive? Yes _X_ No ___**

**8) Is the net income growth rate above 15 percent? Yes _X_ No ___**

**9) Is the debt-to-equity ratio .25 or less? Yes _X_ No ___**

**10) Is the beta less than 1.0? Yes _X_ No ___**

**11) Is the stock price above the 200 day moving average? Yes _X_ No ___**

**12) Are insiders buying more than selling? Yes _X_ No ___**

**13) Is the company buying back stock? Yes ___ No _X_**

**14) Does the company have intrinsic value? Yes _X_ No**

**15) Passes Screening = Answering Yes 12 or more times**
**Fails Screening = Answering No more than 3 times**
**Pass** _X (12 questions yes)_ **Fail ___________**

Alon USA Energy Inc. is a great example of a growth stock that fits the criteria that we are looking for. Notice how the company passes the screening test with a score of 12. All of this data can be found at MSN Money or Yahoo Finance. MSN offers a free stock screener service on its investing homepage that you can use to help find stocks that match our criteria. You simply customize the screener with our settings and the system will search through every stock in the market until it locates good growth stocks. The screener doesn't search for everything we want to see, but it can help you narrow your search down to the stocks that show potential. You will have to do some digging by yourself.

It only takes about 20 minutes to screen a stock. The toughest part is determining if the company has intrinsic value. If you don't understand what the company does, it is going to be difficult to figure out if the company has intrinsic value. Stick with companies that are easy to understand. Alon USA Energy has intrinsic value because they own over 800 miles of oil pipeline networks in the Gulf Coast region. They produce over 70,000 barrels of oil per day and lease their pipelines to other companies. Their product and services are always in high demand. You have to break each and every stock down like this to make sure the stock isn't trendy. Chances are that if a company provides a product or service that is always in high demand, they have intrinsic value. The new Apple iPod is not an example of a product that will always be in high demand.

Once the screening portion is complete, we still have to run our stock through the buy worksheet to make sure the market conditions are ripe for buying. If the stock passes the stock screening test but fails to pass the buy worksheet, you cannot buy the stock. A technology stock will never pass the buy worksheet test. It's not a coincidence that Warren Buffett never bought an internet technology stock during the 1990s boom. He understood that these kinds of companies don't have true intrinsic value. We want to invest like Warren Buffett because his strategies are proven effective.

## Completed Sample Buying Worksheet

**Buying Questions:**

**1) Is the prime rate currently below 9%? Yes** _X_ **No** __

**2) Does the stock pass the screening test? Yes** _X_ **No** __

**3) Is the company in a non-competitive industry sector that doesn't require constant innovation to remain successful?**
**Yes** _X_ **No** ___

**4) Does the company have significant intrinsic value?**
**Yes** _X_ **No** ___

**5) Is the stock selling at a discount to earnings?**
**Yes** _X_ **No** ___

**6) Do the company strengths outweigh the weaknesses?**
**Yes** _X_ **No** ___

**Company Strengths:** No insider selling. All buys.
Record-breaking earnings last Qtr.
Reduced debt by 100.5 million dollars.

**Company Weakness:** Price-to-book value high for industry.
No stock buyback program in place.
______________________________

**7) Buy stock if you answer yes to all the questions.**
**Don't buy stock if you answer no to any question.**

**Investor Decision: Buy** __X__ **Not Buying** _____

As you can see, the buy worksheet has given us permission to purchase Alon Energy USA. The buy worksheet is kind of like asking your wife for permission to buy something. It keeps you in check and only allows legit purchases. The prime rate is good for stock buying and the stock passed the screening test. We established that the company has significant intrinsic value, and that the P/E ratio is way less than half the net earnings growth. This stock is definitely selling at a discount to earnings. And last, but not least, the company strengths outweigh the weaknesses.

An example of a major company weakness would be an ROE way less than 20 and a high debt-to-equity ratio. Use common sense when deciding if a company has too many weaknesses compared to strengths. Most companies will not pass the screening test if they have too much debt because they will fail multiple portions of the test.

Once we purchase stocks for our portfolio, we have to periodically monitor them to make sure they are still performing like they were when we bought them. We should monitor our stock performances about every six months. Sometimes, companies hit a rough patch and their stock suffers. It is not our intent to buy and sell stocks like crazy. Warren Buffett holds stocks for years after finding good ones. The sell worksheet will help us determine if a stock needs to be sold. We're only going to sell if something catastrophic happens. In order for us to sell, the prime rate has to jump above nine percent. The company also has to fail the screening test, take on significant debt, suffer a growth slow down, or lose intrinsic value.

Don't worry about what the market is doing on an everyday basis once your portfolio is in place. You're in this for the long haul. Great companies with good fundamentals and intrinsic value will come out smelling like a rose in the long run. Utilize the stock screening guide and buy and sell worksheets to your advantage. You can be confident knowing that you will create a portfolio of winning stocks when you correctly analyze a stock.

# CHAPTER 8
# DIVERSIFYING YOUR DYNAMITE PORTFOLIO

I think Forrest Gump said it best; "life is like a box of chocolates, you never know what you're going to get." The same is true for investments. You can the call the 1-800 physic numbers, get your own crystal ball, or summon the investing gods with your Ouija board, but you still won't be able to predict how your investments will perform in the future. To counteract this dilemma, we have to be diversified in our investments. Don't put all your eggs in one basket because you'll likely end up with egg on your face.

Many people try to time the market to gain an edge. *Market Timing* is when people try to predict future market directions by examining market data. Some companies promise fabulous returns and often have great short-term results, but fizzle in the long-term. It is impossible to accurately predict the short-term direction of the stock market. Occasionally, the market goes against the grain and wipes out any short-term market timing gains.

It is possible to predict the long-term direction of the stock market. The stock market has always risen during the long-term and will continue to do so as our nation grows. Please refer to the historical stock chart below.

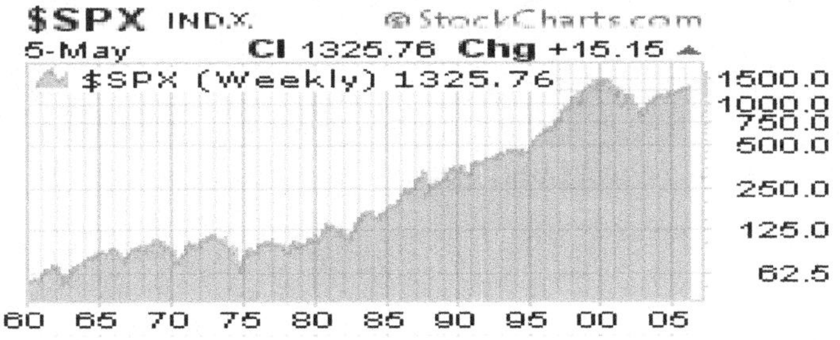

The S&P 500 historical stock chart shows the overall upward advance of the stock market since 1960. Notice the small ups and downs, but the steady progression upward. Would you rather bet on long-term steady growth or short-term market ups and downs? Be a smart investor! Intelligent investors have diversified portfolios, stay for the long-term, and shift their portfolio around when the prime rate hits the target zones we discussed in chapter five.

## Self-Regulating Portfolio

For those of you out there who want your portfolio to be diversified and require no intervention on your part, you can set up a self-regulating portfolio. A self-regulating portfolio consists of three types of funds, divided as follows: 60 percent of your investment money deposited into an S&P 500 fund, 20 percent deposited into an international stock fund, and the remaining 20 percent deposited into a bond fund. The theory behind this organization is that you own shares of stock that are always performing well. For example, if U.S. economy is bearish, your bonds will perform well. No matter how the world markets are behaving, one of your three funds will generally be performing well. Refer to Table 8-1 below.

**Table 8-1 Self-Regulating Portfolio w/t $400 per month**

| Ticker/Fund | Percentage | Amount |
|---|---|---|
| VFINX (S&P 500 Fund) | 60 | $240 |
| VGTSX (International Fund) | 20 | $80 |
| VBLTX (Long-term bond Fund) | 20 | $80 |
| | | Total = $400 |

I chose Vanguard index funds as an example in Table 8-1. They have very low expense ratios and you can purchase them from almost any brokerage. This is an excellent way to organize your portfolio. You can also set your Roth IRA up like this. A Roth IRA can consist of more than just one fund, but you can't contribute more than the yearly max when you combine them all together. If you want to set your Roth IRA up like this, you cannot deposit more than $333.33 (2006 contribution limit) into the three funds. You'd want to deposit $200 into the Vanguard 500 index fund, $66.66 into the Vanguard total international stock index fund, and $66.66 into the Vanguard long-term bond index fund. Make monthly deposits into these funds by dollar-cost averaging.

## Conservative Approach

A conservative portfolio is one that doesn't involve a lot of risk. Investors who have a conservative approach buy investments that match benchmarks. They want to match the overall market return. All of us should have a conservative approach towards our retirement accounts. We want our investment portfolio to be diversified. You can never go wrong with index funds for the cash and bonds. Utilize a high-yielding money market account for your cash position. As the prime rate rises and falls, shift the percentages.

**Table 8-2 Conservative Investment Portfolio**

| Stocks | Bonds | Cash | Prime Rate |
|---|---|---|---|
| 60% | 25% | 15% | < 9% |
| 25% | 60% | 15% | > 9% |
| 10% | 20% | 70% | > 14% |

## Moderate Approach

A moderate portfolio is designed to take a little more risk in return for possible higher returns. This portfolio basically puts a higher percentage towards stocks. Somebody who has extra money to invest because their retirement account has reached the contribution limit is a good candidate for this kind of portfolio. Don't use this approach for your retirement accounts!

**Table 8-3 Moderate Investment Portfolio**

| Stocks | Bonds | Cash | Prime Rate |
|---|---|---|---|
| 760% | 20% | 10% | < 9% |
| 35% | 55% | 10% | > 9% |
| 25% | 15% | 60% | > 14% |

## Aggressive Approach

An aggressive portfolio is heavily invested in stocks. An aggressive style should only be used by people who have contributed the maximum to their retirement account, and have 20 or more years before the money will start to be withdrawn. Basically, this portfolio is sacrificing large cash and bond positions in return for long-term future stock growth. The aggressive portfolio doesn't really follow our prime rate chart very well. Its main objective is to grow like the historical stock chart. We know that stocks always rise over the long-term. A young investor can't go wrong with an aggressive portfolio because they have time on their side. The same holds true with index funds for this portfolio as it does with the moderate and conservative approaches.

**Table 8-4 Aggressive Investment Portfolio**

| Stocks | Bonds | Cash | Prime Rate |
|---|---|---|---|
| 80% | 15% | 5% | < 9% |
| 70% | 20% | 10% | > 9% |
| 60% | 15% | 25% | > 14% |

## Individual Stock Diversification

Some of you may be wondering how you can diversify with individual stocks. Those of you who want to pick your own stocks instead of buying an index fund need to know how many individual stocks to own to get an accurate representation of the market. Many investors debate about how many stocks they should own. I'm going to tell you to buy as many as you can accurately keep track of. Don't get too crazy here. Having 10 to 20 stocks representing multiple industry sectors that pass the screening test is enough to get an accurate representation of the market.

Don't buy a bunch of stocks from the same industry sector. Find stocks from multiple industries. I try to find the leaders from each industry that pass the screening test. You want stocks that are leaders in their industries. The key is to make sure your stocks are properly screened and that the major industries get a chance to represent your portfolio. Sometimes, there will be a plethora of stocks available that pass screening, and other times, it will be slim pickings.

So how much do you invest in each stock? I recommend buying equal amounts of each stock. If you have $3000 to invest, and you successfully screen 10 stocks, buy $300 worth of each stock. Periodically add to each stock position over time.

## Diversification Summary

So hopefully, everything is starting to come together for you now. We've covered a lot of information so far, but you should have a pretty good idea what you need to do. Build a portfolio that is diversified in stocks, bonds, and cash. Monitor the prime rate and shift your investments around as it dictates.

Never put all your eggs in one basket, no matter how good a stock looks on paper. I've known guys who said they met the hottest girl they've ever seen only to realize that she had an Adam's apple. Looks can be deceiving!

If time is on your side, build an aggressive portfolio. Time is your most powerful wealth-building weapon. Always refer back to the historical stock chart when you think stocks are not the right investment. There will be lots of dips and dives, but your portfolio will grow over time. Don't let people discourage you from buying stock. There are many people out there who have no idea what they are talking about and they have never studied the historical data. As Will Ferrell says, "Keep on Truckin'!"

# CHAPTER 9
# PERIODIC PORTFOLIO MAINTENANCE

The investments in your portfolio are constantly changing. They change faster than a teenage boy's voice during puberty. Mutual fund expense ratios, stock fundamentals, and overall return performance change over time. Some investments are more stable than others, but it's important that you check the stats on all your investments to make sure that they are meeting your expectations. You may have a well-balanced portfolio set up one year, and five years later everything is out of whack. We want to prevent this from happening by going through a checklist every three to six months. Six months is adequate, in my opinion, but I prefer to check my portfolio every three months. I check everything when I get my quarterly statements in the mail. Refer to the Table 9-1 Portfolio Checklist.

**Table 9-1 Portfolio Checklist**

1. Is your portfolio balanced with the correct percentages in stocks, bonds, and cash, based on the current prime rate?

2. Do your mutual funds, index funds, or ETF funds have a higher than 1.5 percent expense ratio?

3. Are your mutual funds, index funds, or ETF funds still meeting their benchmarks?

4. If you have individual stocks in your portfolio, do they still pass the screening test?

5. Run any individual stocks that are struggling through the Sell Worksheet to see if it's beneficial to sell or hold.

The most important part of the checklist is the first step. Always make sure your investments are allocated correctly, based on the prime rate and what type of portfolio you have. Remember that your investment portfolio contains a retirement account and a non-retirement account. The retirement account should be conservative and your non-retirement account should be either moderate or aggressive.

Question number two references your funds expense ratios. Sometimes, mutual funds increase their expense ratios because they start advertising more, or whatever. Keep an eye on these fees. These fees are listed in the funds *prospectus*. A prospectus is a pamphlet that is distributed by your fund that lists all the fees and types of investments that the fund owns. Always read the prospectus before investing in the fund. You can often find these online.

The next area of concern deals with funds meeting their benchmarks. If a fund claims that they want to match the performance of the S&P 500, they need to do just that. This is why I recommend buying index funds over other mutual funds. It makes no sense to buy a fund that underperforms their benchmark.

The last two areas on the checklist are for those of you who have individual stocks in your portfolio. Obviously, you still have to make sure your stock passes the screening test. Use some common sense here though. If the market is bearish, overall stock performance will struggle. Give a stock a chance if its fundamentals are still sound.

## Stay in the Loop

It's a good idea to follow the news headlines about stocks you own. Every so often, I will check the key developments or recent news sections on MSN Money or Yahoo Finance. Discover what the companies' visions are for the future so that you can determine whether or not their intrinsic value is increasing or decreasing. I'm not saying that you have to get e-mail alerts and stalk the company employees like the paparazzi, but you should know if a company plans to expand to a new country. After all, you do own a portion of these companies.

## Shifting your Portfolio Strategy

Eventually, you will have to pull the reins back on your moderate or aggressive portfolio approaches. It's not a good idea to be investing aggressively when you're 65 years old because you don't have time to recover from a major market correction. When you get within 10 years of needing to withdraw the money, stop investing with a moderate and aggressive approach. Your aim should be to conserve your principle at this point in time.

## Dodging a Bullet

Reviewing your portfolio every three to six months will prevent diseased funds or stocks from devastating your overall return. It's kind of like giving a penicillin shot to your portfolio. However, there shouldn't be too many changes in the short-term. Purchasing low expense ratio funds and buying stocks that pass a screening test help alleviate too much portfolio turnover. Play it cool like the man of steel, and learn how to dodge bullets by completing the portfolio checklist at least twice a year.

# CHAPTER 10
# SMART INVESTMENT ADVICE

We've come all the way from financial suicide to creating a dynamite portfolio. My intent is for you to be able to pick up this book and find your way to financial freedom no matter what your current position or knowledge level is. Anybody can do it. However, it will take a little longer for those of you who may be deep in debt. If you're stuck in a hole, get up, dust yourself off, and develop a plan to climb out. Your financial well-being is dependent on your ability to take control and work a plan. Exhibiting control with your finances is not temporary. It's a way of life. You now have a map at your fingertips. Use this book and research other resources to develop a plan that works best for you. In this chapter, I've included a few tips to help you out and keep you from stumbling along the way.

## Searching for the Holy Grail

All of us have seen the late-night infomercials on TV that promise riches beyond your wildest dreams. Hurry! You must act quickly because this offer expires in 30 minutes. Don't you just love those? The truth is that most of these get-rich-quick schemes are garbage. You'll end up getting wrapped up in a pyramid scheme and spending tons of money on concentrated cleaning products, motivational CDs, and seminars. That is only the beginning. These types of businesses make the majority of their money selling motivational materials. Who really needs a lifetime supply of concentrated soap and vitamins? The Dollar Tree sells name-brand laundry soap for 99 cents. People are kidding themselves if they think these companies have intrinsic value.

I've tried a few of these get-rich-quick schemes out before. My favorite scam was the Don Lapre 1-900 dating line service. For a small nominal fee of about $400, Don set you up with dating line service that never worked right. Customer service would never answer their phone and trouble tickets went unanswered. Lo and behold, his company went out of business. Would it surprise you if I told you that he's selling vitamins now?

## Day Gambling

I'm sure most of you have heard of *day trading*, or at least know of someone who has done it. Did you notice how I said that in the past tense? Day trading is a form of trading that involves buying and selling shares of stock in very short periods of time with the intent of turning a quick profit. Day traders often end up broke because they are gambling their investment money and paying huge brokerage fees. It's impossible to predict short-term market performance! You have a better chance of chugging a gallon of milk without puking than being a successful day trader. People will feel tempted to day trade during future bull markets because trading online is so easy. That was the fad in the late 1990s until the technology burst. I'd rather go to the casino instead. The casino may give you a complimentary meal unlike a brokerage house.

## Penny Stocks

Investing in *penny stocks* can be another dangerous undertaking. Penny stocks are stocks that are valued at less than five dollars a share. People get greedy and think they can stock up on shares because the stock is so cheap. The stock is cheap for a reason! These companies usually have terrible fundamentals and are saturated with debt. Sometimes, there is a good penny stock out there, but they are extremely difficult to find. I've yet to find one that passes the screening test. Warren Buffet once said that he would rather own one share of a solid company instead of 100 shares of a penny stock. The most successful investors ignore the temptation of buying penny stocks, and focus on finding companies with solid fundamentals.

## Jumping on the Bandwagon

There are many services out there that rate individual mutual funds based on performance. The most popular one is Morningstar. They assign up to five stars for the best funds and one star for the worst performing funds. It's kind of like getting a smiley face sticker next to your name in fourth grade after you did your book report. People get wrapped up in these rankings and jump back and fourth in between funds that have the best rankings. It's not worth it.

A few studies have been done about highly ranked Morningstar funds and they all came to the same conclusion. These funds fare no better than other funds over the long term than other funds do. Actually, their overall performance lags over time. A fund can be ranked number one for a couple of years, and then they'll be ranked towards the bottom. You're better off sticking to an index/ETF fund, or going with a balanced fund with a low expense ratio.

## Risk Tolerance Levels

Some of you may be a little leery about investing aggressively with your portfolio. Don't invest aggressively if you're not comfortable doing so. If you're one of those types who wake up in the middle of the night in a cold sweat worrying about your stock performance, an aggressive portfolio may not be right for you. Don't forget that all of us need to have a conservative retirement account, but whatever you set up for your non-retirement account is up to you.

Another thing that helps people to stop worrying about their portfolio is to ignore daily stock market news reports. Warren Buffet doesn't pay attention to daily reports because they can be distracting. Pay attention to the market when you are doing your periodic portfolio maintenance and ignore it the rest of the time. The more educated you are about the market, the more comfortable you will become. The topic can be very boring at times, but there's something about making large sums of money that can be motivating.

## Options, Futures, and Commodities

I can sum up this section in just a few words. Stay away from these! *Options* are contracts that give an investor the right to buy or sell shares of specific companies at predetermined prices for limited periods of time. *Futures* are contracts to buy or sell shares of specific companies at a future dates. *Commodities* are anything that comes out of the ground, like corn, wheat, oil, or metals. Unless you are actively engaged in studying these types of investments, you will almost certainly lose money. I have known a few people who have been successful at trading options, but they do their homework and use software programs to help the screening process. The average investor should avoid these at all costs.

## Life Insurance Investing

One of the first investing scams that I fell for was life insurance investing. A fast-talking salesman once talked me into starting an investment plan that combined life insurance and a retirement account all in one. It sounded like a great idea because I thought I was getting the best of both worlds. First of all, I didn't need life insurance because I was 18 years old, and I was single. Secondly, I didn't realize that I was paying for the life insurance premiums, the commission for the salesman, and the mutual fund 12B-1 expense fees. These types of investments are called "annuities" and they combine a death benefit plan with a mutual fund. The fees are so ridiculously high that the account performance suffers in the long-term. Never combine investing with life insurance!

If you have one of these accounts, close it as soon as possible. I immediately called the company I invested with to cancel my account as soon as I found out how the business really worked. They'll charge you an early withdrawal fee, but you'll end up saving a ton of money in the long run.

## Wills and Trusts

Eventually, you're going to kick the bucket and your significant others are going to be eager to get a slice of your nest egg. Many people think that this magically happens, but the government steps in to make the decisions if somebody doesn't have a will or trust in place. A will allows you to call the shots. It's a legal document that directs the disposal of your property. Not having a will leaves your estate in shambles. It's not like you'll care because you're dead, but everyone who's left behind will have to deal with the consequences.

A trust is another tool you can use to leave your estate in the right hands. A trust grants a beneficiary of your choice the right to distribute your property as you see fit. Make sure you trust the beneficiary to make the right decisions on your behalf.

So how do you set up a will or trust? The best thing you can do is set up an appointment with a licensed attorney. Some people do wills online, but they lack some legal power. Do some research and find a reputable attorney who specializes in wills and trusts. You want to make sure your will is legit and notarized by the proper authority. Don't take any shortcuts when you are drafting a will or trust. The state will find loopholes in your document if it's not done correctly. The Better Business Bureau can help you screen reputable attorneys and law offices. They can be reached at http://www.bbb.org.

## Insurance

Whoever thought of making insurance a regular part of our life was evil and a genius all wrapped in one. Paying for insurance is annoying because most of us rarely use it, and when we do need to file a claim, we generally get the runaround. The bottom line is that all of us need insurance to help protect our assets. A disaster can wipe out our emergency and savings funds. You need to avoid sustaining any battle damage to your savings portfolio.

Let's take a look at the big picture for a second. If you live in an area that is ravaged by hurricanes, tornadoes, floods, or earthquakes, it's definitely a good idea to make sure your insurance covers you. Why would you even want to risk it? Most of the victims from Hurricane Katrina did not carry hurricane coverage. These people had to start over from scratch. Can you imagine being 10 years from retirement and having to start over? That's not a pretty picture.

## Last Call

Hopefully, all of you have learned something to help make your journey through life more prosperous. Some of you are going to take this information in stride and create a workable plan. Others will put this book to the side and miss a golden opportunity to live wealthy. Whether you decide to make a financial lifestyle change, or continue down the path of debt is up to you. They both require work on your part. One is positive and the other is negative, but the workload is about the same. People deep in debt spend just as much time figuring out how to get loans or increase credit card limits as wealthy people do screening no-load mutual funds and diversifying their portfolios. It's all about how you focus your efforts. Take the path of least resistance and save yourself from drowning in a sea of debt!

# REFERENCES


**Chapter 2. Controlling the Madness**

Orman, Suze, *The Road to Wealth* (Berkley 2003) A Comprehensive Guide to Your Money.

**Chapter 3. The Golden Rule**

Clason, George S., *The Richest Man in Babylon* (Signet 1988).

**Chapter 4. Organizing your Financial Picture**

Bielagus, Peter G., *Getting Loaded* (Penguin 2003) Make a Million While You're still Young Enough to Enjoy It.

**Chapter 5. Deciphering the Financial World**

Investor's Business Daily, *Guide to the Financial Markets* (John Wiley & Sons 1996) Profit from financial news.

Givens, Charles J., *Wealth Without Risk* (Pocket Books 1995) How to Develop a Personal Fortune without going out on a Limb.

Investor Words, *Most Comprehensive Financial Glossary* (Jul 2006) http://www.investorwords.com.

MSN Money Research, *Stock Charts* (Jul 2006) http://www.moneycentral.msn.com.

## Chapter 7. Educated Decision-Making

Lynch, Peter, *One Up On Wall Street* (Fireside 2000) How to Use What You Already Know to Make Money in the Market.

Hagstrom, Robert G., *The Warren Buffett Way* (John Wiley & Sons 1997) Investment Strategies of the World's Greatest Investor.

## Chapter 8. Diversifying your Dynamite Portfolio

Graham, Benjamin, *The Intelligent Investor* (Harper Collins 2003) The Definitive book on Value Investing.

Historical Chart Gallery, *Stock Charts* (Jul 2006) Simply the Web's Best Financial Charts. http://www.stockcharts.com.

# ACKNOWLEDGMENTS

I'll spare you the cheesy Academy Award style acknowledgements, but I have to thank a few people who helped me make this book a reality. First of all, I'd like to thank my gorgeous multi-talented wife, Jodie, for helping me organize my thoughts and proofread for hours on end. Secondly, I wanted to thank Columbia College professor, Dr. Alesa Lightbourne, for her professional insight and editing skills. And last, but not least, I want to thank the U.S. Navy for starting a financial specialist program to help educate Sailors about financial planning.

Made in the USA
Monee, IL
08 November 2026

67377474R00059